THE RED LETTER PARABLES

Introducing
Jesus
As Master Storyteller

Bob Palumbo

And the disciples came and said to Him, "Why do You speak to them in parables?" Jesus answered them, "To you it has been granted to know the mysteries of the kingdom of heaven, but to them it has not been granted." [Matthew 13:10]

THE RED LETTER PARABLES
Introducing Jesus as Master Storyteller
by Bob Palumbo

ISBN- 13: 978-1978020368
ISBN- 10: 1978020368

Editing: CBM Christian Book Editing

Interior Design/Layout: CBM Christian Book Editing
www.christian-book-editing.com

Printed in the United States of America

ACKNOWLEDGMENTS

As anyone who has ever read a great book might guess, most authors do not work alone. This one sure doesn't. I might be the one typing the manuscript and coming up with the chapter titles and storylines, but I have had a tremendous amount of teaching, help, encouragement and friendly criticism in my life. And I am thankful for every morsel of it. I would not be me without it.

I am going to rattle off a bunch of names, here, of the people who have made large deposits of love, support and encouragement into my life. They have played a big part in what this book has become, just by being in my life. My wife, Lauri Lee, my daughters, Tarra Oppewall, Jessica Veselenik, Bobbi Jean Palumbo and my son, Philip Palumbo, Barbara Coates, George Loper, Pastor Ken Roberts, Pastor Jim Mindling, Pastor John Jacobs, Pastor Ken Bublinec, Pastor Terry Whittenburg, Mark Higgins, Jonathan Guzzo, Bill Cornish, Grace Hejnal, Lloyd Crawford, Chad Hoffman, Gary Haden and Maralyn Janoch. All these amazing people deserve more credit than I am giving them here, but I pray they all know how much I appreciate them.

I also want to mention a handful of authors who have no idea how much they have meant to me, but it was a lot. C.S. Lewis, Frederic Buechner, Charles Swindoll, Max Lucado, Watchman Nee, John Eldredge, John Piper, J.R.R. Tolkien, Rabbi Jonathan Cahn and so many others who have enlightened and enriched me along the way. And I thank them all for that.

Thank you, also, to all the fine folks at Christian Book Marketing. It has been a joy to work with you all.

And last, but certainly not least, I thank God, without whom none of us would exist in the first place. All glory and honor is Yours, Lord. Thank you, Jesus, for allowing me to be Your witness.

TABLE OF CONTENTS

INTRODUCTION

S tories. Who doesn't love a great story? It doesn't matter if you are three-years-old or ninety-three, stories never cease to entertain, captivate and enlighten us. And they come in all shapes and sizes. Some stories are heartfelt; some are heroic, while others are light or humorous. And the storytellers in our lives can be as varied as the stories themselves. Great stories often come to us through parents, grandparents, teachers, pastors, friends and co-workers...not to mention the more prevalent sources of the modern age...books, television, movies and the Internet. Even video games are story-based, although they're more of an interactive type where by playing them, we can affect the outcome. But they are modern stories, nonetheless, that are greatly loved, as well.

Nowadays, when we do find a classic story in a book, a movie or on television (like "Rocky," "Star Wars," "Harry Potter," and many more), they become so popular that those who produce them often come up with one or more follow-ups. We have come to know them as sequels, or prequels, or a sequel to the prequel...or maybe even a prequel to the sequel (a.k.a. . .the original story. . . lol). And why not? If we loved the first offering, why would we not be anxious to gobble up stories about what happened after the original story took place, or before it? If it works, stick with it.

One of my favorite movies to watch was called, "The NeverEnding Story." What a concept, a story that never ends. Although, they may not have thought that one through, because the title of the first one pretty much negates any justification for a sequel. But bless their hearts; they did try anyway, twice really, without much success though. The point remains, however, we humans love our stories. Always have and always will.

In the Bible, of course, stories are very much a part of that greater "neverending story." We have Noah and the Ark, Abraham and Isaac, David and Goliath, Daniel and the Lion's Den and the story of Joseph. There's Jonah and the Whale, Song of Solomon and one of my favorites, the story of a young Moabite girl named Ruth. Imagine a young woman who loses her husband, follows her mother-in-law back to her homeland of Bethlehem, goes to work in the fields for a wealthy landowner who is a relative of her mother-in-law, ends up marrying the wealthy landowner and becomes part of the bloodline that brings forth the long-promised Messiah who was to one day appear (and He did) to ultimately deliver Israel. Pretty hard to top that "rags-to riches" saga, right? Yet, the Bible does.

So far, I haven't even mentioned the story of Jesus Christ. It has been called "The Greatest Story Ever Told." A child who became a King. A Savior who came down from Heaven to redeem those trapped under the bondage of sin and death. Then, through His own suffering, death and resurrection, He becomes the ransom that sets the captives free, so that they may live forever and never die. It has all the elements necessary to make it "a story for the ages."

There is a beautiful and hopeful beginning, followed by the usual struggles of life and, in this case, some very unusual ones to say the least. Then, it all culminates with the most powerful plot and point of all, a life interrupted too soon, which is finally resolved by this interrupted life miraculously being restored victoriously and the chief antagonist paying the ultimate price for his crimes. And there you have it, a very happy ending. And, in case I forget to mention, you definitely want to keep an eye out for the sequel to this one. I have reason to believe the sequel is going to be even more incredible than the original story (that is pretty rare, I know, but in this case, I believe it's true).

What I found interesting enough to become the premise for writing this book, however, was that this Jesus, the central character of this amazingly true story, was a lover of stories, Himself. Jewish tradition has always leaned heavily on great stories. The Rabbis of Old had books full of them. And those stories have been handed down through the generations and are still loved and embraced by those of the Jewish faith today. So, there is little doubt that Jesus grew up hearing and cherishing those same stories. In fact, He told many thought-provoking stories during His ministry here on Earth, and now has come to be revered by many as maybe the greatest storyteller of all time. He certainly has my vote. My goal here is not to just come to know these stories that Jesus told better, but to really get to know our Lord and Savior as a Master Storyteller. We will be not only looking at the stories themselves, but why and when He chose to tell them.

The stories which we will "zoom in" on here, you know them as parables (from the Greek word "parabole" and the Hebrew word "masal"). They are best defined as "side stories" or stories that "come alongside" to help illustrate or clarify a larger point or issue. Think about the movie, "Mary Poppins." There is a very famous song from that movie called, "A Spoonful of Sugar." The takeaway from the words of that song might say it best, "A spoonful of sugar helps the medicine go down." I think that is about as clear an explanation of what a parable is as anything I can come up with. A parable is the sugar that helps us to grasp or swallow the more important truth or lesson…the medicine, if you will.

I have decided to call this book, "The Red Letter Parables" (like the red letter editions of the Bible, I've always loved those) because the focus is on the parables that were the actual words of Jesus Christ, Himself. There were certainly other parables in the Bible, which were not uttered by Jesus. In Judges 9, we read about "trees making a king." In 1 Kings 20, there was "the smitten prophet." In Isaiah 5, we hear about "wild grapes." In Ezekiel 17, you have the story of "the great eagles and the vineyard." And probably the most famous Old Testament parable of all, recorded in 2 Samuel 12, where Nathan the prophet confronted King David concerning his sin with the beautiful Bathsheeba by telling him a story to get his attention. So again, I am quite sure Jesus knew all of these ancient parables quite well because He grew up hearing them read in the Temple and, more importantly, He was God in the flesh. Jesus knew, very well, the power of a well-told story. So, it is not surprising that He would use this skill quite often as He walked among us.

Interestingly, in doing the research for this book, one thing struck my interest. Most of the lists of "The Parables of Jesus" only point to the ones recorded by Matthew, Mark and Luke, or what is called "the Synoptic Gospels." They seem to overlook what I think are some pretty important ones that were only recorded in the Gospel of John. So, with your permission, I would like to include a few of them, as well. I may be stretching the traditional definition or criteria for what is considered "a parable" a bit. But, I hope you don't mind. I think they are important to the overall storyline.

I also think the parables in all four Gospels are helpful to the bigger picture of understanding how and when Jesus used them. Not just the individual parables as separate teaching moments, themselves, but when these stories are connected (like pixels in a digital photograph), do they help to convey a super-parable, one on a larger and more eternal plane? Do they add weight to the Good News of the relationship between God and man and how He chose to redeem us to Himself forever? I have no doubt they will, but it might be fun to do some digging and see for ourselves. Are you in?

I do, however, want to mention at the outset here, that there are hundreds of great books written on the parables of Jesus, by authors with much greater expertise and insight into the Bible than I, all of whom do a wonderful job of explaining what these stories were meant to convey, not just to those who listened first hand, but to those of us who came after. But it is my view, that if Jesus is the Master Storyteller, as I believe Him to be, then the individual parables should be pretty easy to understand, all by themselves, and not require tons of deciphering. So, I do not want to spend too much time on all of that.

My goal here is to walk through these precious stories, arranged mostly chronologically here (I have taken a few liberties for the sake of the flow of the book), to see what can be learned from not just one parable or another, but also why Jesus grouped them together as He so often did. Most Bible experts point to "Five Main Discourses" where most of these parables were shared. The most famous one, of course, was the Sermon on the Mount where He rattled off quite a few in rapid succession. But I found He did that often, and my guess is there was a very deliberate reason why they were grouped together as they were. Also, the order in which they were told, chronologically, may prove to be revealing in its own way. It is my belief that nothing God does is happenchance or coincidental.

So, I believe we will see the same type of divine orchestration, here, as we did in my first book, *Unlocking Creation*, and I am very thankful that you have decided to come along for the ride as we now look at *The Red Letter Parables* and get to know our Lord Jesus Christ in a whole new way. . . as the Master Storyteller of all storytellers.

NOTE TO THE READER: Going back to the earlier reference to a digital photograph again, in each chapter we will be looking at a particular parable in two ways. "Zooming In" will be looking briefly at the parable, itself, as it stands alone. "Zooming Out" will then tackle the question of how it may fit into the bigger picture, to reveal the real "neverending story." My hope, again, is that it will enhance our understanding of the true nature and character of God, the Father, the Son and the Holy Spirit, and reveal just how far He was willing to go to show His love for us, His children.

PART ONE

"All Things New"

"Behold, I am making all things new."

Revelation 21:5

STORY ONE

"Saving the Best for Last"

And Jesus said to her, "Woman, what does that have to do with us? My hour has not yet come." His mother said to the servants, "Whatever He says to you, do it." [John 2:4-5]

ZOOMING IN

So where, then, should we start? I think it would be good to start, thinking chronologically, at the Wedding at Cana, which is recorded in John, Chapter 2. You may be asking yourself, "Why would we start there? Jesus did not speak in a parable at this wedding. He performed His first miracle there." And you would be right. But if a parable is "a side story that clarifies or points to a greater truth," then this entire event could be seen as a "parable without words," if you will. I think it is an important part of the greater story that pretty much sets the tone for all the parables that will follow.

Jesus spoke in parables, basically, for two reasons:

1)   For those that have eyes that see, they reveal deeper truths.

2)   For those who do not see or believe, it points to their blindness.

I like to think of it as a password, of sorts. In the "Old Days" (before the Internet), you would be asked for a password before being allowed to enter a place that was for "members only." If you did not know it, you did not get in. So, a parable was a way to separate "the sheep from the goats," in a way. Not that Christ needed to see that, He already knew His sheep and His sheep knew Him. But, to the Disciples, and to the others who would hear Him speak, it often revealed a disconnect, either within themselves or in those around them. Just the mere presence of the Son of God could be very polarizing. These stories that He told and the miracles He performed, only made it more so.

So, this wedding was attended by Jesus, His mother, Mary, and some of His Disciples, which in and of itself, paints a very symbolic picture that may not have been understood by those who were there at the time. But that is also another key aspect of a parable. They are not only meant to be seen and understood by those who were present and within earshot. They also provide teaching and clarity for those of us who were to come after. When the headwaiter says, "Every man serves the good wine first...but you have kept the best for last," his words became sort of a revelation or parable for us, even though it was puzzling to him. Unknowingly, he was pointing to "a departure from the status quo." He was announcing a new and different way of doing things.

If Jesus Christ was nothing else, He certainly was a drastic change from the old ways. What was done before, was simply no longer good enough. In Him, all things became new. So much so, that Jesus Christ, Himself, became the only thing that matters in the end. He was not just "the new kid on the block." He is ultimately the "neverending story." Serving the best wine last, as the headwaiter pointed to, became the side story, here, that clarifies what was actually happening. He might have thought he was just speaking about how wine should be served at a wedding, but it was so much more. Don't you just love how God uses innocent bystanders, without them even knowing, to speak to us on His behalf at times? I do.

This beginning of His signs Jesus did in Cana of Galilee, and manifested His glory, and His disciples believed in Him. [John 2:11]

16

That is why I felt this was such a good place to start, because the turning of the water into wine spoke of something much greater. It signified a new beginning, a change in the program. And it was a change initiated by God (although most did not know that yet). And that symbolic gesture, when Jesus obliges His mother (Honor thy Father and thy Mother) by doing what she asked Him to do, even though as He said, "My hour has not yet come," He is clearly signaling to His Disciples and those with eyes that see, "We are not in Kansas anymore. We are now on a new and different path." And as I said, this miraculous event set the tone for every miracle and parable that followed.

But another interesting thing happens in John, Chapter 2. Although most lists of "The Parables of Jesus" do not include it, Jesus actually did speak in a parable for the first time (chronologically) and John records it here in the same chapter, not long after He made the "best wine" for the wedding feast.

Jesus answered them, "Destroy this temple, and in three days I will raise it up." [John 2:19]

You know, until I actually started to do my research on this book, I never really noticed that this one chapter included these two dramatically different pictures of Jesus. The first, was the loving and compassionate one, obeying His mother and turning the water into wine, so the guests at this special wedding could enjoy themselves. And secondly, the righteous side of the Son of God cleansing His Father's House. Talk about a dichotomy. Here within a handful of verses, John shows us the compassionate nature of God and the righteous, just side of God Almighty.

To portray God as simply one or the other would not be an accurate picture of who He is. Jesus often displayed both sides, as well as many other divine attributes, to those He met. Some refer to these two sides as the "maternal nature of God," that reveals the loving and nurturing attributes and the "paternal nature of God," which shows us the strong and more justice-oriented side of God's nature. Some have even gone as far as using this to explain why God had to create both male and female, since He was capable of being both and we, of course, are not. But I will leave that discussion for another day.

17

So, it is here, I believe, that Jesus chooses to speak in a parable for the first time. And it is very important, because once again, sometimes Jesus spoke in parables to believers, or to His Disciples, to reveal His relationship to His Father. But other times, He spoke in parables to those who did not recognize who He was, knowing they would not understand what He meant until much later. This was one of those times, as He of course was referring to His own body, which would eventually be killed and brought back to life on the third day, not the physical Temple. But the Jews did not understand that, at least not yet.

ZOOMING OUT

What an incredible chain of events that unfolded in John 2, and I could not help but step back and wonder how this will all tie into the "bigger picture" of the Gospel of Jesus Christ. Here in one amazing chapter, we see a miraculous event, the changing of water into wine signaling the beginning of a new day. And it would change everything that followed it. God had "saved the best for last." The wine would not change back into water at midnight, as everything did in the story of Cinderella. No, the Wedding of Cana announced a permanent change, one with eternal ramifications.

On the other hand, the parable about "destroying the temple" spoke about the end of His earthly story, not the beginning. So, in one chapter, John points to two separate events near the beginning of the earthly ministry of Jesus Christ. One that announces a new beginning and another that foretells of His eventual end. How amazing is that?

As we go through this book and look at dozens of examples, this same pattern will hold true. Many will reveal His compassionate nature, others will show us His righteous indignation and yet, others will point to another new beginning, the Kingdom yet to come.

No one can tell a story quite like a master storyteller, so I think it is appropriate that we should prepare to be amazed.

STORY TWO

"Nic At Night"

Jesus answered and said to him, "Truly, truly, I say to you, unless one is born again, he cannot see the kingdom of God."
[John 3:3]

ZOOMING IN

As I mentioned in the Introduction, I am strongly of the opinion that Jesus spoke in parables in all four gospels, not just the Synoptic Gospels. And some of the ones that were only recorded by John, as I see it, are pretty darn important to the Gospel message, as a whole. There may be no better example of this, in my opinion, than in John Chapter 3, where Jesus encounters a Pharisee named Nicodemus. Nicodemus comes under the darkness of night to speak privately with this teacher who is causing quite a stir among the Jews.

So, let me just get right to it; I believe John 3:3 is a parable, or at least part of a parable (since there are more word pictures to come in this conversation). Nicodemus is telling Jesus that they perceive He is from God because no one could perform the miracles He does unless God is with Him. But when Jesus answers Nicodemus, this is where things get a little dicey. Many people use John 3:3 as a verse that confirms the need for us to become "Born Again Christians." While I am not suggesting that we do not have to be born again, born of the Spirit, to be saved and receive eternal llife in Christ (because I believe we do). I am not fully convinced, however, that this is what Jesus was talking about here.

I have been taught, as others have, that to rightly understand a statement, it's best to make sure you understand what was said leading up to the statement. Context matters. In this case, the discussion begins by Nicodemus saying, "We know that you are from God. . ." Jesus then responds by saying, "Unless one is born again, he cannot see the kingdom of God". It sounds to me like Jesus is saying, "For you to be able to see that, you would have to be born of the Spirit". Now, if that is what Jesus meant, then He is complimenting Nicodemus on being spiritually aware, not telling him that he needs to be saved. Big difference.

But the reason I believe this is a parable, is because Jesus, as Master Storyteller, uses something we are all quite familiar with, the physical birthing process, to illustrate a spiritual need that everyone of us shares just as much as being born physically, if we are to inherit eternal life. So, in a roundabout way, the simple response from Jesus to Nicodemus does speak to the question of eternal life and Heaven. But, I think He did it in a way that complimented Nicodemus as much as it challenged him. But Nicodemus did not fully understand what was happening, again, at least not yet.

"Do not be amazed that I said to you, 'You must be born again.' The wind blows where it wishes and you hear the sound of it, but do not know where it comes from and where it is going; so is everyone who is born of the Spirit." [John 3:7,8]

Let me be careful here, I do not put any stock in the assumption that Jesus is saying here, "Just like with the wind, people who are born of the Spirit have no idea whether they are coming or going either." Okay, that was a little charismatic humor there, forgive me. I just had to toss that in, to lighten things up a bit. This is serious stuff we are talking about. But I do think this is another example, from the Gospel of John, of Jesus speaking in parables. He is clearly using the wind as a way to explain the things of the Spirit. Sounds like a "side story" to me.

But is Jesus suggesting to Nicodemus that, like with the wind, you might be able to sense the presence or influence of the

Holy Spirit, but you may not correctly discern where it is coming from or where it is going? Remember, Jesus was misunderstood by many (especially the Jewish hierarchy) to be of the devil when He performed miracles. So, I think He was cautioning Nicodemus, who was a High Priest, not to be fooled. But also, that he needs to be willing to "think outside of his religious box" to fully understand what is happening. This point is more fully confirmed when Jesus says the following words.

"Are you the teacher of Israel and do not understand these things? If I told you earthly things and you do not believe, how will you believe if I tell you heavenly things?" [John 3;10, 12]

This is a classic example of another way in which Jesus used parables. Sometimes, He used them to reveal things to those who believed and were seeking answers. Other times, He used them to show unbelievers how much they didn't know. With Nicodemus, I think it was more the latter. On one hand, Jesus was complimenting him for sensing something special was happening, spiritually, and coming to Him for answers. But at the same time, I believe He was telling him that he would never find the answers he was looking for under the Old Covenant, following the Law and the ancient traditions of the Jews. That old dog could no longer hunt, if you will. All things had become new.

ZOOMING OUT

In the previous chapter, the Wedding at Cana ushered in a new day, a new everything, really. The Messiah had arrived, in the flesh and in power, and nothing was going to stay the same. Even the age-old idea of birth was about to take on a new and fresher meaning. Humans need to be spiritually born, not just physically born, to encounter God and find eternal life. Just offering the same old sacrifices and keeping the feasts, year after year, that was not going to suffice any longer.

At this point, I would really like to highlight one more amazing detail from this story, if I may. It is right in this very same chapter, John 3, and from this very same conversation between

Nicodemus and the Lord Jesus that we get the most famous and most quoted Bible verse of all time:

"For God so loved the world, that He gave His only begotten Son, that whoever believes in Him shall not perish, but have eternal life." [John 3:16]

For most of us, I am sure this popular verse needs no explanation. We have heard this many, many times. But I would have loved to have seen the look on the face of Nicodemus, when this person who he called "Teacher" refers to Himself as the Son of God. The actual phrase, "Son of God", was never used in the Old Testament, although there were verses that implied a relationship between God Almighty and a son. So, for Jesus to refer to Himself as the Son of God, that had to set off his internal heretic alarm system, presuming he had one, of course. Most folks, in that day and time, would have considered this to be blasphemy.

And if that wasn't concerning enough, He goes on to say that by believing in Him, not Jehovah or the Father or even obeying the Mosaic Law, that someone referred to only as "whoever" in John 3:16 (not just a Jew) shall not perish but have eternal life. Poor Nicodemus's head had to be spinning. Who was this person, that upon meeting someone for the first time, declares that He, Himself, is the Son of God and that by believing in Him one might be saved, even someone who is not a descendant of Abraham? I could only imagine the level of his confusion. This teacher, if that is what he thought Jesus was, just challenged everything he believed in his whole life.

Nicodemus is mentioned a few other times in the Gospel of John, once sticking up for Him at the Sanhedrin and he is also mentioned assisting Joseph of Arimathea in giving Jesus a proper burial. So, we do not know for sure if he was truly (at least in his heart...maybe not openly) a believer. But he apparently had great respect for our Lord and Savior, to say the least.

What Nicodemus learned, from his meeting with Jesus, was that we all need to be born both of water (physically) and of the Spirit (spiritually). And while that may be a bit confusing to us, just as it was to Nicodemus, it all comes down to faith. It begins with seeking God, as Jesus said in Matthew 6:33, ". . . *then all*

these things shall be added unto you." Just as a man and a woman have to become intimate, for life to be generated and a physical birth to take place, we have to become "intimate with God" for a spiritual birth to come about, as well.

I think it is safe to say that the meeting of Jesus and Nicodemus, one night in Jerusalem two thousand years ago, further advances our suspicions that Jesus came to boldly proclaim that, in Him, all things...even the concept of birth, have become new. And no doubt, many were not going to welcome these new revelations with open arms, especially the most religious ones of that day and time.

STORY THREE

"Thirst No More"

"Everyone who drinks of this water will thirst again; but whoever drinks of the water that I will give him shall never thirst; but the water that I will give him will become in him a well of water springing up to eternal life." [John 4:13-14]

ZOOMING IN

If you love a great story, and as we talked about in the opening chapter, "Who doesn't?" then John Chapter 4 is a great one to dig into. It has all the makings of a classic story. A man meets a woman for the first time (it was just the two of them, the disciples had wandered away). The woman is from the wrong side of the tracks (Samaria) and has a reputation and this man is aware of it. But He is drawn to her anyway; in fact, He loves her. Okay, He is God, so He loves everyone. Yeah, I probably did get carried away with the drama, there, maybe just a little bit. But it was true, He was drawn to her and He did desire to have a relationship with her, one not of this world.

So far, in these stories from the Gospel of John, we have heard about a wedding and a miracle of turning water into wine. We have heard about a High Priest of the Jewish faith, coming to Jesus under the cover of night, to try to get some answers for himself about this controversial teacher that everyone is talking about. And now Jesus meets a woman from a place that is not thought of highly among the Jews, who also has a checkered past (and present, actually). We hear of water becoming wine, being born for again a second time, the Spirit being like the wind, and now we hear of water that causes you to never thirst again. Is there a common theme in all these stories? I would say, "You bet your sweet bippy."

Everything that Jesus has done, here in the early part of His earthly ministry screams loud and clear, "Nothing is the same. Everything has changed." It's like Jesus is saying, "Forget everything you thought you knew, before today. I have now come in the flesh and what I bring with Me, has never been revealed before." Uh-oh. Now what?

Did Jesus judge this woman, because of her checkered past? He certainly seemed to know all about it. No, He did not. What He said to her had everything to do with making a change. From that moment forward, nothing He said to her was about the past. Sure, He let her know that He knew of her past. But He was only interested in changing her future, just as He is with you and me. If we truly come to Him, truthfully and sincerely, everything changes from that moment forward. There is no looking back.

But there was also a second parable, in this chapter. This one He shared with His disciples:

"I have food to eat that you do not know about." So, the disciples were saying to one another, "No one brought Him anything to eat, did he?" Jesus said to them, *"My food is to do the will of Him who sent Me and to accomplish His work."*

When the Disciples had come back, they found Jesus talking with this despicable Samaritan woman, but they didn't dare question Him? They let it slide.

But they did notice that He was tired and probably hungry, so they said to Him, "Rabbi, eat." But instead of saying, "Sure, what do we have?" He chose to not respond directly, but took things in a different direction.

One of the aspects of being a Master Storyteller, is recognizing when you have the full attention of your audience. Now, if we go to a movie or a play, or pick up a book, obviously we are in the mood for a good story. But, for storytellers that look for those moments of spontaneity in real time, that spring into "story mode" whenever opportunity knocks, they tend to be constantly aware of the degree of interest of those around them. Who was better at this than Jesus Christ?

So, the Lord seizes the moment here, by teaching the Disciples that for Him, there is more to "finding nourishment" than just eating and drinking. There is also "spiritual nourishment" that comes from doing the will of the Father and spending time in His presence. We are not just talking about "saying grace," or "giving thanks for the food," here. No, it is so much more than that.

Just as He had shared with the Samaritan woman at the well, there was not only water that causes one never to be thirsty again. There was also food that is not of this world that nourishes in ways beyond that which we get from bread or meat. Although, I am not sure the Disciples fully understood what He was referring to, but it was a theme they would hear again and again.

ZOOMING OUT

From that city, many of the Samaritans believed in Him because of the word of the woman who testified, "He told me all the things that I have done." So, when the Samaritans came to Jesus, they were asking Him to stay with them; and He stayed there two days. Many more believed because of His word; and they were saying to the woman, "It is no longer because of what you said that we believe, for we have heard for ourselves and know that this One is indeed the Savior of the world." [John 4:39-42]

So, this look at the parable of John Chapter 4 ends the first group of parables from Jesus as recorded by the Apostle John (we will touch on a few more later, as well). But you may be asking yourself, "Why did he choose to start off this book with stories from three chapters of John, when most experts do not include parables of Jesus from the Gospel of John?"

In the beginning, I said that the definition of a parable was "a side story" something to enhance or clarify a greater point within a discussion. And I said that I would be probably taking some liberties by including examples that are not on most lists. That is what I have done with these first three examples from John.

27

Plus, I also mentioned that we would be going somewhat chronologically to see if there might be a greater message underneath it all, in the timing and the order in which Jesus chose to share these "side stories." These three examples, in most chronologies of Jesus, came before the more widely accepted parables in the Synoptic Gospels of Matthew, Mark and Luke.

I really think there was some significance to these three chapters coming first. They announced, quite clearly, that "All things have become new." As I said earlier, water became wine, there was now a second birth and it now seems possible to never thirst or hunger again, if you drink and eat of the "things from above," which are not of this world.

This new program He was announcing, early on through John, was greatly "outside of the box" compared to any religious perceptions that were embraced before "the Word became flesh and dwelt among us." And to be sure, this was not going to be welcomed by the "religious or business as usual" crowd. Oh no, they saw all of it is as a very serious threat to their traditions and their livelihoods. They were not going to take it "sitting down," as we know all too well.

There is one more point I would like to make before moving forward. As I mentioned earlier, Jesus knew when He spoke these parables, that they would not only be heard (or read) by the people He was directly talking to. No, He knew that these stories would be recorded and read (and loved) by people of all generations, for centuries to come.

So, we need to remember that when we read stories like His discussions with Nicodemus, or the woman at the well, He was not speaking thusly, just for their benefit...but for ours, as well.

STORY FOUR

"The Doctor Is In"

But when Jesus heard this, He said, "It is not those who are healthy who need a physician, but those who are sick. But go and learn what this means: 'I desire compassion, and not sacrifice,' for I did not come to call the righteous, but sinners." [Matthew 9:12-13]

ZOOMING IN

Moving on from the gospel of John to Matthew's account in our chronological walk through the parables of Jesus Christ, we come to this memorable statement from our Lord. The Pharisees had just criticized Him to His Disciples for *"eating with tax collectors and sinners"* and Jesus, overhearing what they said, came back with this famous response, *"It is not those who are healthy who need a physician, but those who are sick."* What an interesting comeback, since no one was talking about anyone being sick.

Just before this, Jesus had called a man who was a tax collector, named Matthew (also referred to as Levi in Mark's gospel), and Matthew apparently invited Him to his home to eat dinner along with some others, including the Disciples. Similar to the situation with the woman from Samaria, tax collectors were also frowned upon. They were looked at as greedy and even shady characters. The Pharisees were making the point that if this Jesus was a righteous and moral teacher, why would He be willing to be seen with those of such a questionable nature?

"... for all have sinned and fall short of the glory of God." [Romans 3:23]

One of the reasons I like our Lord's response here, is that I detect (my own opinion here) a little sarcasm on the part of Jesus. He makes a comparison between the healthy and the sick...and then correlates it to the righteous and the sinner. In a way, is he suggesting the tax collectors and sinners are the sick and the Pharisees are the healthy and righteous ones? That is what I perceive in Jesus' statement and that is why I sense some sarcasm. He knows the Pharisees are not without sin and He knows that they are well aware of that fact, too. I see Jesus in this story just letting them know He sees behind their religious facades.

That might be one of the greatest departures from the old traditions that Jesus brought to light with His "all things new" message. In the past, there were perceived levels of goodness or righteousness (or the lack thereof) within the ranks of the nation of Israel. You had the likes of Melchizedek, the High Priest that the writer of Hebrews talked about as a forerunner of Christ when he wrote, *"Now if perfection was attained through the Levitical priesthood, what further need was there for another priest to arise according to the order of Melchizedek."* He was considered special because for one, he was of the bloodline that eventually brought forth the Messiah (Jesus claimed to be that Messiah openly to the woman at the well when He said, "I am He."). And secondly, Abraham (who was the great-grandfather of Levi, from which the Levitical priesthood came) paid tithes to Melchizedek. It was in the Jewish tradition that the lesser party paid tithes to the greater, so that suggests that Melchizedek was ranked higher than the Levitical priesthood on the "holiness scale" of the Jewish faith, which was all about rank and authority and the money and power that went with it.

Then there was Caiaphas, who was considered a High Priest, but not on the level of Melchizedek. He was the reigning High Priest of the Sanhedrin at the time of Christ's ministry (the Sanhedrin was the "Court of Seventy-One," which was made up of seventy High Priests and one High Priest that chaired this council of priests). This was like a Congress, of sorts, ruling on and interpreting all sorts of issues and problems. Then, beyond that, you had the Elders and the Scribes. They performed the more menial tasks of the priesthood. So, you see that even within the religious realm, there were many various levels of religiosity and implied honor.

The people, unfortunately, were truly just the pawns or peons in those days. They pretty much lived and worked to serve the upper echelon. Jesus came, among other reasons, to "level the playing field."

"For there is one God, and one mediator between God and men, the man Christ Jesus" [1 Timothy 2:5]

Let's think about this for a minute. If we, indeed, are ***"all sinners and fall short of the glory of God" [Romans 3:23]*** and now Jesus Christ is the only mediator between God and mankind, that leaves a whole lot of "big shots and middlemen" whose jobs might be on the religious chopping block. They clearly knew He posed a threat to their ways of doing things. And Jesus wanted them to know He knew their time had passed. After all, if all things were indeed new, then what need was there of a High Priest to offer sacrifices on behalf of the sins of the people? That, of course too, had changed; the Jews just did not know it yet. Jesus, as Messiah and Savior, following His death on the Cross and His resurrection on the third day, permanently took the place of the High Priests for all of mankind, not just the Jews, when He became as John the Baptist prophesied, ***"the Lamb of God who takes away the sins of the world." [John 1:29]***

I think we now can more fully appreciate the sarcasm of Jesus saying, ***"It is not for the healthy that the physician comes, but for the sick."*** We are all sick, even the priests. As Isaiah wrote, ***"We all like sheep have gone astray." [Isaiah 53:6]*** Sin, from the very beginning in the Garden of Eden, had "levelled the playing field" by leaving every single human being who would ever live in need of a Savior. But it wasn't until this Lamb of God arrived on the scene, to pay the ransom for us all, that the world finally began to pay attention.

31

ZOOMING OUT

This short little parable in Matthew 9 loomed large, in the bigger picture, I think. Not only did it provide further confirmation to what we saw at the Wedding of Cana, with Nicodemus and the woman at the well, that certainly "all things had become new" and that Jesus brought hope to the formerly hopeless ones at the bottom of the social ladder. This parable clearly served notice to "the powers that be," that their days were numbered.

No longer was there going to be a "top down" hierarchy, with regards to the things of God. Through His only begotten Son, not only did He remove the need for a social ladder, in the first place, because everyone was on the same level in the eyes of God, a sinner in need of redemption. He highlighted the fact that those in a position of authority are not there to be served by those underneath their authority, but rather they are to serve others, not themselves.

Do you see an underlying theme starting to develop, here? First, the water changes into wine and it is announced that through Jesus "the best wine came later." Then we learn that we are no longer only to be born of the water, but also the Spirit (the best coming later, once again). And the woman at the well found out that there was a type of water, that if anyone drank it, they would never thirst again. So again, Jesus revealed even a new type of water, the best coming later again. And now, we see the religious hierarchy being challenged by a new type of High Priest that is "later and greater" than the former, more temporary type and the sacrifices they offered. Jesus became the permanent solution that would never leave us wanting or thirsty. Again, we see the Lord was "saving the best for last."

Thank You, Lord.

STORY FIVE

"Here Comes the Bridegroom"

And Jesus said to them, "The attendants of the bridegroom cannot mourn as long as the bridegroom is with them, can they? But the days will come when the bridegroom is taken away from them, and then they will fast." [Matthew 9:14-15]

ZOOMING IN

Now, we see the Disciples of John the Baptist coming to Jesus and asking Him, "Why do we and the Pharisees fast, but Your disciples do not fast?" So, not unlike the Pharisees, even John's disciples were seeing that Jesus and His disciples were playing by different rules and they wanted to know why? It's the old "goose and gander" logic at work. You know the game, "Hey, if we have to do this stuff, what makes you so privileged that you don't have to?" They had not fully realized that Christ was "the game changer." John the Baptist understood, but apparently his disciples were not yet convinced.

Immediately, Jesus goes into Master Storyteller mode. He asks them a hypothetical question, giving them something tangible to compare it to (which is exactly what a parable is, a side story or illustration, to teach or clarify).

He is not speaking directly about Himself, here, but indirectly He is making a point in such a way that they can relate. These disciples of John, and certainly the Pharisees, knew the process by which a Jewish man and woman would become betrothed (or engaged as we call it) and eventually married. They knew that the prospective bridegroom would have to leave his home, travel to the home of the girl he wanted to marry and formerly ask the father for permission, bringing him a suitable offering and, of course, propose to the woman of his dreams. And usually, he did not go alone, but had a group of his close friends travel with him as witnesses. But they also knew that, after that, the bridegroom would return to his home and begin to prepare a place for his bride to come and join him, after the wedding feast was completed.

The disciples of John fully understood all these Jewish marriage traditions, no doubt. But the fact that Jesus chose to indirectly refer to Himself as a bridegroom, at this time and in this situation, raised some eyebrows, I'm sure, because they also knew the prophetic significance of the Bridegroom and they knew that Israel was portrayed, prophetically, as the Bride. I am guessing there was plenty of whispering going on between these disciples of John, as to what Jesus was actually saying.

Was He referring to Himself as the Messiah? Could anyone really be that bold or arrogant? I am of the opinion that they also felt a little threatened by the arrival of Jesus Christ. Their days, as disciples of John were numbered, as well. John the Baptist came to "prepare the way" for Christ. Once this Lamb of God, as he called Him, was revealed, there was no longer a need to prepare the way. The One "who was to come" had arrived. His work, and theirs, was done.

ZOOMING OUT

As with everything that Jesus said and did in those days, I'm sure word of this claim He was making about Himself travelled fast. If there was Twitter, back then, He would have been the #1 trending topic every day, I'd guess. There was a buzz, to say the least. So, you can bet word of this filtered back very quickly to all of the religious and political "big wigs," along with all the other stories of these "outside of the box" claims Jesus was making regarding Himself. I can almost hear them saying, "Wow, what an ego this guy has." Discussions were already beginning, in secret (I am sure), of what should be done to put an end to these heretical claims Jesus was making.

But why did Jesus choose this moment and this place to use the illustration of a bridegroom. And how, if it all, did this tie in the bigger picture of "all things becoming new?" Now, here, we see Him revealing a new picture of a bridegroom, one that has nothing to do with a man or a woman, but rather a relationship between the One True God, the God of Abraham, Isaac, and His beloved chosen ones, Israel.

As for the timing of this parable, in Matthew 9:1, it says, "Jesus crossed over the sea and came to His home city (which most believe refers to Nazareth). But there is some quirkiness in how this chapter was written, if many of the chronologies of Christ are correct. The calling of Matthew, in Matthew 9, happens quite a while before Matthew 9:1 where Jesus comes back to Nazareth. And Matthew's calling supposedly happened in Capernaum, but the chronologies suggest the dinner that followed was probably in Nazareth, at a later moment in time. Also, based on the chronologies again, a whole lot happened between 9:9 and 9:10, including the Sermon on the Mount and the parables of Matthew 13, all of which we will cover later.

But for the sake of the storyline here, I wanted to keep the parables of Matthew 9, like Matthew did, together. They just fit in better here. I hope you will bear with me on that.

So, we now have a new and better wine, a new birth, a new type of wind, new water that permanently quenches our thirst, a new and greater physician and now a new type of bridegroom.

Maybe there is, after all, an underlying theme and a greater story being told here by this Master Storyteller they call Jesus.

STORY SIX

"Patches"

"But no one puts a patch of unshrunk cloth on an old garment; for the patch pulls away from the garment, and a worse tear results." [Matthew 9:16]

ZOOMING IN

As I mentioned earlier, one of the most interesting things I found when I first started digging into the "when, why, where, who and what" of these word pictures we call parables, was how many times these stories or illustrations came in bunches. That actually reminds me of a humorous story that a dear old friend once told me. He told me that his young daughter told him that she really liked carrots, especially "the bunch variety." She thought that since we buy carrots in bunches, that they grew that way, in bunches, sort of like grapes. I loved it. Kids say the darndest things, do they not? Art Linkletter had it right.

So here in Matthew 9, we have some parables, "the bunch variety", the type that come in clusters. Now, here, we have a parable about a bridegroom, immediately followed by this one about "sewing" (not to be confused with "sowing," that one comes a little later). And next, we will get back to wine and how it is stored and transported in these things called "wineskins." But right now, I want to dive into this problem of old cloth and new patches. This one is a little puzzling to me. Let me tell you why?

First of all, silly me, whenever I have read this parable in the past, in my mind, I would automatically picture an old pair of jeans that I remembered from my youth. Blue jeans were often patched when they got a hole in them, sometimes with an "iron-on patch" (remember them?). Of course, that is before tattered and "holey jeans" (not "holy" jeans) became fashionable.

The problem with my assumption is there were no such things as blue jeans in the first century. They did not show up until the 1870's, when Jacob Davis and Levi Strauss partnered up to patent a new kind of durable work pants that Davis made from a fabric called "denim," which he bought from Levi Strauss. Davis made them even stronger by using rivets at the places pants would most likely rip (and you thought that was for appearance...so did I). Davis made these pants, at first, to fill a customer's request for more durable work pants, but they caught on quick and when Davis talked to Strauss about getting a patent on them, they decided to partner up on the venture.

Incidentally, that denim fabric was first developed in France. It was called "Serge de Nimes" or "de Nimes" which was where the name "denim" comes from. This fabric was like a cotton dungaree that was first used to make clothes, unsuccessfully, in Genoa, Italy, which is where the name "jeans" eventually was coined from. See how much I get to learn, not just the readers, from writing these books? Pretty cool, I must say.

So, what kind of cloth was Jesus referring to, that would so easily rip the old fabric, if a new unshrunken piece of cloth was sewn onto that old garment? This seems to go against our prevailing storyline, so far, that applying new things to old things, would make the old things not just better, but like brand new. I needed answers and I needed them fast, if I was going to get this chapter finished. Luckily, you don't have to wait while I do my research. I did it before the book was printed. Your welcome!!

The best descriptions I can find about the garments of those days all seemed to point to most garments being made of either a linen or wool. Usually the linen would be the undergarment, worn closest to the skin, and the outer garment would be more likely be made of wool, for warmth and comfort. Think of the Shroud of Turan, which was the burial cloth that they wrapped the body of Jesus in (presumably). It was a thin fabric, one that would keep someone cool and likely absorb any sweat or bodily fluids that would likely leave a trace. I think it is also safe to say that both these early linens and wools would be nowhere near as strong or durable as the ones which came long after, like denim or heavy cotton-based clothing.

Those early fabrics were also likely to be very prone to shrinking when they were new, much more than the older material which had already shrunk. And we can add that the while the newer fabric would shrink, it was also likely stronger than an older piece of the same fabric. It would make sense, then, that if a patch of new cloth was sewn into an old garment, it is the older, weaker cloth that would rip, just as Jesus suggested. Does it also not point, in a way, to Jesus portraying the "old ways" as weaker, or flimsier than the new ways?

ZOOMING OUT

I think this parable, maybe more than some of the others, goes a long way to show us that a Master Storyteller must not just be able to "weave a good tale," one that holds the interest of the listeners or readers. He or she must know what they are talking about, as well. I think a great story, as riveting as it might be, would fail to "make its mark" if it was not accurately depicting the subject matter that the story evolved from. If not, the audience would likely write the storyteller off as being a phony and not knowing what he is talking about. Obviously, that was not a problem for our Lord and Savior, who knows all things and created all things in the beginning. He had an incredible depth of wisdom and understanding of virtually every subject, which gave Him a big advantage over those who opposed and questioned His authority.

Like Jim Croce sang, they were "tugging on Superman's cape" and "spitting in the wind" when they tried to have a battle of wits with this new so-called "troublemaker." And it usually did not end well for them, either.

The other point that sticks out to me, regarding this second of three parables that came in quick response to John's disciples asking why the Disciples of Jesus did not fast, as they did, was the fact that the "new thing" had the potential to damage "the older thing." Most the other examples of "all things becoming new" pointed to new and different understandings of old perceptions. They did not really pose a threat to the old ones. This one did.

Jesus was telling the disciples of John, and indirectly, the Pharisees, that "fixing the old garment" (religiously speaking) was not going to be good enough anymore. The message that Jesus brought required the old things to pass away or be thrown out, not merely patched. That is why His arrival and message was so polarizing. It pitted the new ways against the old, to a great disadvantage to the old, and it was pretty much signaling the end of their unchallenged power and authority. They were the old garment that would likely be tossed aside, if this new message caught on, and they knew it, which is why they were so greatly troubled by Him.

But Jesus was not quite done, here. He had one more carrot in this bunch for them to chew on. And they were not going to like it any better than this one.

STORY SEVEN

"The Preserving of Wine"

"Nor do people put new wine into old wineskins; otherwise the wineskins burst, and the wine pours out and the wineskins are ruined; but they put new wine into fresh wineskins, and both are preserved." [Matthew 9:17]

ZOOMING IN

As Oliver Hardy would often say to Stan Laurel, back in the day, "Well, this is another nice mess you've gotten me into." It seems the disciples of John the Baptist got much more than they bargained for, when they asked the Disciples of Jesus why they did not fast as they did. Jesus did not just give them one parable, as an explanation, He gave them three. And the last two were more about letting John's disciples know, and anyone else who heard His words, that this new message He was bringing, required the old ways to be thrown out and replaced, not just fixed or updated. A decision needed to be made, on their part, regarding whether they would be willing to turn from the old time-tested ways of the Jews, which they had relied on for centuries. Or seek with all their hearts, this new Gospel of hope and redemption that Jesus preached. It was not an easy decision, I'm sure.

Many have still not accepted the new message, even today, in fact. They might say, "But, what if Jesus was wrong? What if He was a false prophet, another 'flavor-of-the-month' that would appear and be gone before you knew it?" It happened quite frequently, back them. Someone would show up, claiming to have some new revelation or unique understanding of God, only to be later found out to be a heretic, or even worse, a lunatic.

Still, there was something very different about Him. There was a power, an authority, a clarity and pointedness in how He spoke and how He dealt with people, not to mention the miracles and healings. So, what if He was truly the Messiah and they rebuffed Him, thus denying God? What if, as with Noah and the Ark, they missed the boat, and this boat was truly the eternal vessel of redemption we know as Jesus, or Yeshua, which means "salvation."

No, this was no trivial matter. That much was evident, not only to those "with eyes to see," but those who did not as well. They either welcomed Him with open arms and rejoicing hearts or they saw, in Him, the beginning of their own end and began thinking of ways to negate or eliminate Him. But either way, it was not something to "sweep under the rug." It prompted a response from everyone who came into contact with this Teacher and His message.

So now we have this parable, following one about a bridegroom and one about putting a new patch on an old garment. Now, we are back on wine, again. If you have ever attempted to make wine, or even read about the process, you know there is a lot to learn. It is very much an "exact science" and there are certainly right ways and wrong ways to do it, if the goal is to end up with something, eventually, that smells good, tastes good and is something you would be pleased to share with others. So it should not be surprising that how you store the wine before, during and after the fermentation process could be a key to your success, or doom you to failure. This is a "win or lose proposition." A great many batches of wine have been tossed out after months of anticipation because one or more steps were not followed precisely. If you are a person who likes to "wing it," winemaking may not be your calling.

Jesus simply reminds them of something most of them already understood, I suspect. You don't store new wine, that has not yet been fermented, in an old, used wineskin. Like the old garment in the previous story, that had already been shrunk and would not shrink further along with the new unshrunken patch, an old wineskin is not as pliable and does not have the elasticity of a new wineskin. It will not be able to stretch like a balloon, as the wine ferments and gasses form that would require a wineskin to be able to expand to accommodate such an increase in volume. If the wineskin does not have that ability, it will likely burst and both the wineskin and the contents will be of no use to anyone, going forward. Not a desirable outcome, to say the least.

And back in those days, wineskins were often used instead of other containers because the horses could carry them better and some held as much as sixty gallons. So, to make a mistake in this way could be quite costly.

Don't you just love how Jesus had these simple, practical illustrations right at His fingertips, ready to be shared at just the right moment with just the right people? Once again, I don't think any of it is by accident, not even close.

ZOOMING OUT

"And no one, after drinking old wine wishes for new; for he says, 'The old is good enough.'" [Luke 5:39]

I wanted to briefly mention, also, that in Luke's version of this same parable, he adds the verse above. Matthew did not include it. But, I think this one extra sentence that Jesus spoke is "the icing on the cake" to the underlying theme we have been talking about, "all things have become new."

Jesus is adding a bit of sarcasm, again, if you ask me. He is pointing it more directly at the listeners, now. To paraphrase, He is saying, "Do you say, after sewing a new patch onto an old garment and it rips an even bigger hole, 'It's fine. I like having big holes in my clothing." Or after two, sixty-gallon wineskins burst, spilling it all on the ground, do you say, "It's still good. Grab a sponge and let's save as much as we can. Wine is wine. A little dirt won't hurt it." Not hardly. He is telling them that no one, after drinking the old wine, likely says, "Let me try some of this new wine. I think I may like it better." He is saying that it is more likely that once they have become attached to the old wine, the old way of doing things, they won't even be willing to try the new wine.

43

It's like a comfortable, old pair of shoes. You don't even really want a new pair, because you know you will have to go through the whole "breaking in" process again. Who wants to do that, when the old ones feel so good just the way they are. And a "tip of the hat" to my wife is fitting here, because she is the one who talks me into getting new shoes, even when I still love the old ones, because the old ones look like they have been through a war. I would still be wearing twenty-year old shoes, most likely, if it were up to me. So, thanks babe!!

But again, when we zoom out on this parable and the ones that came right before it again, there it is, "all things have become new." And now we are adding to that storyline a bit. You see, it is not sufficient to just fix or repair the old things. Jesus is saying the old things don't work any longer, you need to toss them out, in exchange for the new.

And lastly, He puts an exclamation point at the end of this cluster of stories by saying, "You who have become drunk on the old wine, the old ways. You will likely not want to change and embrace the new. But I am here to tell you, that if you do not, you will be making a deadly mistake."

STORY EIGHT

"Help Wanted"

Then He said to His disciples, "The harvest is plentiful, but the workers are few." [Matthew 9:38]

ZOOMING IN

Here at the end of Chapter Nine of the gospel of Matthew, we come to another one of these "one verse parables," and this one will also be the final one of Part One for our storyline, here, "all things have become new." The Bible teaches, in Proverbs, that when too many words are spoken, transgression or sin is unavoidable. I think we can assume that Jesus fully understood that principle and being the Master Storyteller that He was, He also understood the importance of keeping it short and sweet...and to the point. Longer stories may be more captivating or entertaining, but they are not necessarily better. A great story is one that resonates and sticks with you long after you hear it, regardless of its length. I think this one checks that box, as well.

I also want to mention at the start of this chapter, that this parable is not one that generally shows up on all the more official lists of "The Parables of Jesus." But again, I am using a little looser definition of the word for our study here. I see a parable as a "side story" or a "word picture" to clarify a greater point that someone is trying to convey. I think this one little sentence that Jesus spoke, meets that criteria quite well. So, I have proclaimed it to be, "a parable." I just love this thing they call "literary license."

If I say it is (as the author), for the sake of our discussion, then it is. Sweet.

Jesus had just been through a number of towns and villages, teaching and preaching and healing people of all kinds of diseases. He saw how many people were suffering, physically, emotionally and spiritually. So, He spoke to His Disciples, using an illustration they would understand to help make His greater point. He spoke in a parable, as He often did. But, here is what He was talking about "in plain speak." There are tons of people hurting out there. We need to be about our Father's business and act with urgency and boldness. Time is short.

Certainly, everyone understood that with harvest time, you have a very narrow window of time when things are just the right ripeness. That is why they hire more workers at harvest time. Speed and efficiency matters when time is so critical to having a good outcome. So, portraying the idea of "seeking the lost" as "a ripe harvest" was a perfect fit. It added that sense of urgency that Jesus wanted to convey and the Disciples did not have to think about it too hard. They got it immediately, I'm sure.

But I would like to veer off the path a bit, if I may, and turn the camera around for a moment, off Jesus as the Master Storyteller, and onto the people He was referring to as "the harvest." There used to be this TV show for children out of Canada that my kids would watch called, "You Can't Do That On Television." It was a pretty good show and they did some pretty funny sketches. One of my favorites was a recurring skit they called "Opposite Sketches." These were great. They would take a situation or problem and inject the exact opposite reaction or response from what you would normally expect. And usually, the result was quite humorous. My kids loved it.

I am sure you have probably taken notice of the fact that the Bible is full of seemingly opposite or unexpected premises. The least shall be the greatest. The first shall be last. The meek shall inherit the Earth. God has chosen the foolish things of the world to confound the wise. In my weakness, I am strong through Christ. OK, maybe that last one is not that surprising, at least I hope not, but it still fits here. I want you to think, for a second, about the people Jesus was referring to as the harvest in this parable. They were sick. They were hurting. They were downtrodden. They were, in some cases, morally bankrupt. Jesus called them "sheep without a shepherd."

What kind of harvest is that? Sounds like a lot of "damaged product" to me. What farmer is in a big hurry to harvest bruised fruit or vegetables half-eaten by the animals in the field? But, Jesus still saw them (and us) as a great harvest. And I believe that is because He saw them as they were created to be, not as they were after sin ravaged their lives. He knew that in His Kingdom to come, if they trusted and believed in Him, they would be redeemed and restored to all that God intended them to be in the first place.

Isn't that amazing? Our Lord sees us not as we are, in our fallen state. He sees us as "created in His own image," unblemished and unstained by sin. He sees us as the greatest harvest ever. No wonder we sing, "How Great Thou Art" with overflowing joy in our hearts. Christ sees us as we were meant to be. And yes, He loves us just as we are at the same time. But, He also knows we were not meant to remain this way forever. Do you?

ZOOMING OUT

Remember, in the beginning, I said that many experts who have studied the Parables of Jesus found that they tended to show up in bunches and that they often grouped them into "five main discourses." While my groupings are slightly different, as I mentioned before, I am also grouping them into five unique bunches for a reason. This parable, concerning the harvest, concludes the first bunch.

I think it is unmistakably clear, then, based on the eight separate parables we have looked at so far, that the underlying theme for the first part of His earthly ministry, chronologically, is "all things have become new." We saw water turned into wine, with which I took some liberty (I admit it) by calling it a "wordless parable," because it set the agenda for all the ones that followed. No one had ever seen water turned into wine before, that was totally new, all by itself. But then the headwaiter sort of added weight to it being included by saying, "Who serves the best wine last. Most people serve the best wine first and then the crummy stuff later, after people have been drinking for a while." And look at that, his comments lead us in a great big circle, right back around to what Jesus said about "no one, being drunk from the old wine, will want the new." You get used to what you are comfortable with and you most likely will not want to change.

Then we meet Nicodemus and he finds out that the Holy Spirit is a lot like the wind, we don't know where it is coming from or where it is going. Of course, they didn't have Doppler Radar back then, but now we do know where wind comes from and where it goes (so I'll give 'em a pass on that one). Plus, Nicodemus learns that there is a "new birth" and if that was not enough, he was on the receiving end of, by far, the most popular Bible verse of all time, John 3:16.

Next, we talked about the woman at the well, from Samaria. And she learned of a new kind of water, that once you drink it, you never thirst against. Of course, Jesus wasn't talking about water at all, just like He wasn't really talking about the wind with Nicodemus. That's why they should be called parables, in my opinion, even though most lists do not include parables from the gospel of John. I am not sure why.

Up next, we hopped over to the gospel of Matthew, Chapter Nine and we come across our first "bunch variety" parables. We learned of a new type of physician and got a new understanding of the bridegroom and how it relates to fasting. That was new and different.

That led to the "one-two punch" of the parable of the old cloth (new patch) and the new wineskins (old wine). These two were a little different in that they stipulated that just fixing, tweaking or updating what was done in the past would no longer be good enough. And, of course, that did not sit too well with the folks who were used to drinking the old wine. They liked it, and they really did not want to try any "new wine." Therein lied the problem.

And we finish here with the story of the harvest and how Jesus had His eyes on the "damaged goods." He saw greatness where no one else did. But then, He was Jesus, the Living Word, Immanuel, "God with us."

Immediately after the harvest parable, Jesus placed His calling upon the twelve Disciples. He commissioned more workers. He doesn't just tell stories. He acts.

Did you ever notice that in Matthew 10:1, it says He "summoned (called) His twelve disciples" and in the very next verse it says, "Now, the names of the apostles are these. . ." That is quite revealing, is it not? They went from being disciples (learners) to being named as apostles (sent ones) in just one verse. So much for us saying, "I am not really ready yet. I really don't know enough." Jesus said, "GO." This calling to "discipleship" comes with "on-the-job training."

Oh, one last thing about the "five discourses" or groupings of parables. When I was doing my research, I discovered that at the end of each of the discourses, Jesus would mark the end of it. . . by departing. At the end of each discourse, there is a verse that says Jesus departed. How cool is that?

Here is our first installment:

When Jesus had finished giving instructions to His twelve disciples, He departed from there to teach and preach in their cities. [Matthew 11:1]

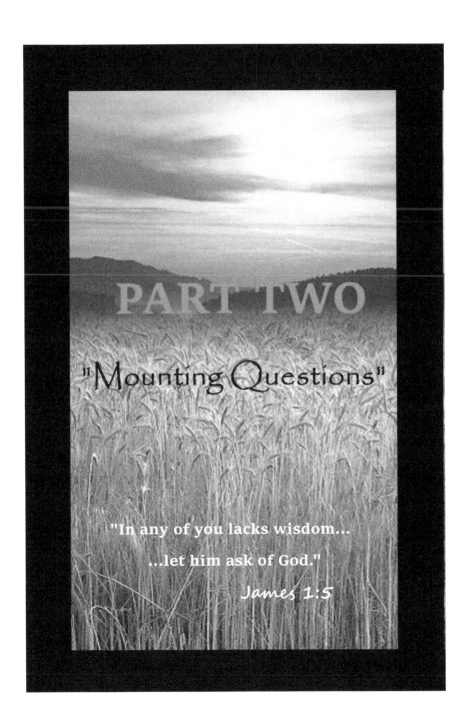

PART TWO

"Mounting Questions"

"In any of you lacks wisdom...
...let him ask of God."

James 1:5

STORY NINE

"A Matter of Taste"

Moving on (backwards actually…don't you love how this chronology stuff works?) from Matthew Chapter 9 to Matthew Chapter 5, we come to another one of these "bunches" of parables, like those carrots we spoke of earlier. Actually, this might be the most famous "bunch of carrots" the world has ever known, The Sermon on the Mount.

Our Lord had been making "quite a splash in the puddle," as they say, for a while now. He has been healing the sick, giving sight to the blind, preaching in the villages, challenging the religious foundations of the day, and to top it all off, He has been making some rather outrageous claims about Himself, causing many to want to hear more and others to become quite fearful, some even to the point of wanting to silence Him, permanently. To say the least, there had been plenty of "mounting questions" about who He really was, His message and what type of response would be appropriate.

If He is a heretic, they cannot allow Him to continue to persuade hearts and minds to turn away from the religious practices they have followed so diligently for centuries, not only to keep people on the right spiritual path (as they see it), but to protect their own livelihoods, as well. Let's face it, the hierarchy of the Jewish faith, in those days, were living quite well off the giving of the faithful. They certainly were not going to give that up without a fight.

So here, as we launch into Part Two of this book, we are going to look at some of the "mounting questions" people had about Him and how it all applied to their own lives. They were beginning to wrestle with beliefs and traditions that they had known since childhood, the sacred things their fathers and grandfathers believed their whole lives. And now, all of this, because of one man and the incredible things He was saying and doing, was "under the microscope."

ZOOMING IN

"You are the salt of the earth; but if the salt has become tasteless, how can it be made salty again? It is no longer good for anything, except to be thrown out and trampled underfoot by men". [Matthew 5:13]

Jesus had begun this historic sermon, on a beautiful hillside overlooking the Sea of Galilee, with what has come to be known as the Beatitudes. Thousands had gathered to hear what He had to say with their own ears. But I would like to comment on that, first, if I may. I always believed Jesus stood on the hillside and directly preached to the masses who had gathered below. But if we read the first verse of Matthew 5, taking it at face value, some questions may be raised about that. It says that when Jesus saw the crowd gathering, He went up onto the mountain (withdrawing from the crowd?), sat down with His Disciples and began teaching them. Wait, so is He speaking to the crowd, or just His Disciples? If He was speaking just to the Disciples, could the crowd hear what He was saying, as well? Enquiring minds want to know?

It says at the end of His discourse, in Chapter 7, that the people were amazed by His teaching. So, you would suspect they could, at least, hear Him. Some have pointed to how well sound travels on that hillside and even extending out to the water. They suggest Jesus could have been talking to His Disciples, directly, but the sound travelled down the hillside in such a way that everyone could hear. Or maybe when Jesus started talking, just to His disciples, someone stood up and yelled, "Could you please speak a little louder, sir? We cannot hear you!!" At which point, maybe Jesus stood up, cleared His throat and started over. I am kidding, of course, but we don't really know exactly. I am assuming everyone could hear Him, one way or another, at least for the sake of our discussion.

The first carrot we see, from this bunch, deals with something quite interesting, if not puzzling to some degree. Salt. And it is yet another of those "one-verse parables" we talked about earlier. Once again, a story does not have to be long to be good, and Jesus certainly had a firm grasp on that concept. So much so, He may have had three middle names, short, sweet and to the point, just sayin'.

I won't spend a lot of time explaining this short, little parable because I think, not only is it somewhat obvious what it meant, it also has been taught a thousand different ways by a thousand different teachers. So, I doubt I can offer much that is totally new. The most common uses for salt, they say, are "to add flavor" to food that might otherwise be bland (this seems to jive with the comment He makes that if the salt loses its flavor, it cannot become salty again). And the other common usage, is as a preservative. Salt is used to keep food from spoiling or going bad. And that would seem to lend itself to the idea that those of us who believe, we are supposed to share our faith with others, to try to preserve their life and keep them from "going bad" (spiritually speaking), as well.

I will only add one more observation to the subject. The term "salt of the earth" could also be pointing to something that is pure, unaltered by man and completely authentic. Think of it as maybe comparing "sea salt" (which is thought to be pure and in its natural form) with processed table salt that is likely not pure or authentic. Again, I don't know which of these interpretations Jesus was primarily pointing to, if any, but they all seem to add some relevance to the story.

I do think He may have been pointing to those who believed in Him as authentic and real. He may also have been suggesting that those who saw God's hand in what He was doing, believed it to be pure and "not contrived by men." I like to think of it as "getting back to the basics" or "wiping the slate clean."

By this time, religious men had added a lot of pomp and circumstance, religious ritual and the human pressures of tradition to the way the Jewish people were supposed to interact with God

Almighty. Jesus, as the Son of God, cut right through all of that. He placed Himself smack dab in the middle of it all, by inferring to the woman at the well and others, that He was the Messiah, the Chosen One of God. And of course, that would certainly seem to follow suit with all the other parables we talked about, as far as revealing a new and better way of approaching God.

I would also suggest the term, "salt of the Earth", was in some way a call to return to simple faith and having a real relationship with God Himself, through Christ, without out all of the trappings and hierarchy of a religious institution. After all, the things God has made, what can we do to improve on them? I do not think many would argue that once humans get their hands on something created by God, and put their twist on it, the result is somehow better. "Hey Jude" is a great song, don't get me wrong here, but in real life it is not often that mankind comes along and "takes a sad song and makes it better."

If God made it, it is pretty much just fine the way it is (at least before Adam and Eve fell into sin...but that is for another day). I'll take the salt of the Earth, or sea salt over processed salt any day of the week. Thank you very much!!

ZOOMING OUT

If the focal point of this second discourse or bunch of parables was about answering "mounting questions," as the title for Part Two suggests, then maybe talking about salt was a good place to start. Most people certainly can relate to what it does for food and see its value as a preserving agent. And I think most would agree that natural salt, the stuff that comes directly from below the Earth's surface is pure, very potent and made by God, Himself, not man.

All of those things would seem to fit quite well with trying to diffuse people's concerns that He was "reinventing the wheel" or igniting "strange fire." As far as I can tell, it certainly seemed to grab their attention, since they stuck around to hear what else He had to say, for what eventually became three whole chapters of the gospel of Matthew. There were a lot of "mounting questions" to come, of course, and our Lord and Savior had plenty of answers.

One interesting side note that I stumbled on as I was digging around on this subject, was an old English phrase, "below the salt." It seems, if someone was referred to as "below the salt," they were common folk, or of low standing. The phrase dates back to the medieval table customs. During those times, salt (which was a valued seasoning) was placed in the middle of a dining table and the lord and his family were seated "above the salt" (favored) and other guests were made sure to be seated "below the salt."

While this illustration may have not been in the mind of the Son of God at the time of His message on that hillside two thousand years ago, I think it would fit in with His message that no longer would there need to be this perception of some folks being favored or revered and others being lower and of less value, "the haves and the have-nots" if you will. Rather, Jesus was saying we are all equal in the eyes of God. You are not "above the salt" or "below the salt."

You are the pure salt, if you believed in Him, He might say. And if you not only believed in Him yourself, but sprinkled some of that salt on others, as well, it could certainly "add flavor" or meaning to the lives of the people you touch or have an influence with, and it could also "preserve their lives" into the "kingdom to come," as well.

Now that is a mouthful...all from one little verse in Matthew, is it not?

STORY TEN

"The Advantage of Height"

"You are the light of the world. A city set on a hill cannot be hidden; nor does anyone light a lamp and put it under a basket, but on the lampstand, and it gives light to all who are in the house. Let your light shine before men in such a way that they may see your good works, and glorify your Father who is in heaven." [Matthew 5:14-16]

ZOOMING IN

Just one verse after Jesus compares us, as believers, to something that forms deep below the surface of the Earth (salt), yet emerges from that darkness as something both valuable and flavorful, He now is taking us to "higher ground." Isn't that just like our Lord? A limitless God who understands the earthly limitations we constantly must contend with. And, of course, He also has full knowledge of both extremes, height and depth, since He created every inch of it, from to the toppest top, down to the bottomest bottom.

Hills were used for all kinds of things over the centuries. Armies preferred to build their forts on higher ground. It allowed them to more quickly see if an enemy was approaching. I'm sure you have heard the term, "uphill battle." So, obviously, you did not want to be the army charging up a hill to engage your enemy. You would much rather be the ones charging down the hill from a fortified location. We would only have to look back in our own history, to World War II and the Normandy Invasion (or "D-Day" as we call it), to fully appreciate the disadvantage that lack of elevation causes on the battlefield. The Allied forces, over 150,000 strong that day, were said to be like "sitting ducks" as they had the unenviable task of fighting their way up from the water's edge on the beaches of France, to overtake the German fortifications on the surrounding hillsides. Our troops eventually gained control of those areas, taking that part of France back from the Nazis, mostly due to the sheer number of the invading allied forces. But, many thousands were lost in the battle along the way.

"Higher Ground" is not just desirable for waging war, or just the name of a classic Stevie Wonder song. It is also the best place to build a lighthouse. With regards to the horizon, a lighthouse situated on higher ground would be seen from much farther away by approaching ships than one which was built closer to sea level. That is also why some lighthouses are taller than others, of course. The taller the better, unless you were the one who had to walk up those steps every day. There were no elevators back when many of those older lighthouses were built.

There has always been another interesting perception, when it comes to the height of certain things like a lighthouse or a city, or the lack thereof. It had to do with the term "city on a hill" being thought of as a virtuous city or one that had flourished to the point of being admired in some ways. A person of "high morals" is generally preferred over someone of low moral standards and I think it is from this perspective that Jesus shared His thoughts about a "city set on a hill" and how it is not easily hidden.

When we are given a position of prominence or authority, whether in the political realm, the church or even in a workplace or family, once you achieve an elevated status in one way or another, the spotlight (or cameras nowadays) is always on you. Things you may have been able to get away with before, are now out in the open and fair game, as they say. It goes with the territory, so be careful what you wish for, if you are intent on climbing that social ladder.

Higher status means higher visibility, and that also comes with the need for more accountability. Jesus certainly understood that. An interesting dynamic, here, is that on one hand this man who claimed to be the Messiah, or from God, seemed to be suggesting that the religious hierarchy the Jews used to gain power and influence for themselves had run its course. Now that God had sent His Son to be the Mediator between God and man, as it says later in 1 Timothy 2:5, there was no longer a need for a High Priest. Jesus, now, is the only High Priest we will ever need, much to the dismay of Caiaphas and the others who were greatly troubled by the radical claims He was making. So, you might think He would say that being a "higher up" was not always a good thing.

But on the other hand, our Lord seemed to be encouraging those who were gathered on that hillside that they should desire to be someone that others look up to, people of virtue and people who shine the love of God on those around them. He implies here, that God does not shine His love on us or bless us, just for ourselves, but that we might also be beacons of light and love to others, as a lighthouse on a hill. We should not keep it hidden or to ourselves.

It is like the words of that classic Reba McEntire song, "Love Isn't Love ('til you give it away)," so simple, yet, so profound.

That's the Master Storyteller at work, is it not?

ZOOMING OUT

As I step back from this parable and take another look at it, this time from the frame of reference of the "big picture," I am quickened by another peculiar part of this little story:

"Let your light shine before men in such a way that they may see your good works, and glorify your Father who is in heaven." [Matthew 5:16]

If I am reading this right, it sounds like He is instructing us to feel free to let our own light shine before people in such a way that they may see how good we are. That doesn't sound right. It is not like Him, in my mind, to encourage us to "put on a show" for others in such a way as to make ourselves look good. That is what the Jewish and Roman bigwigs did all the time and Jesus did not seem all that fond of their behavior. Is this a change of thinking, here, or am I missing something?

61

Let's keep reading, so we don't jump to conclusions, here. The last part of this parable ties it up quite nicely and even puts a bow on it, "**. . . and glorify your Father who is in heaven.**" So in the end, Jesus brings it right back around to where He started. The goal is to bring God glory, not ourselves.

But, He kind of does it in a roundabout way, does He not? He starts by telling us "You are the light of the world." Wait. Jesus is the light of the world, not us. But, here He is saying we are, too. And then, at the end of this masterful story, He says we should let our light be seen by men that they may see our good works. All of this had to have many in the audience wondering where He was headed with these somewhat radical statements.

Well, like the name of Part Two implies, there were plenty of "mounting questions" concerning this Jesus of Nazareth. And for a lot of folks, this sermon on this hillside overlooking the Sea of Galilee did not fully answer them. In fact, for some, it only raised more questions, I would think.

But it does point to another important aspect of this Master Storyteller. His stories, His parables, they were meant to draw those who were His, closer to Him. While at the same time, they were designed to repel those whom He knew would never come. And once again, as the Son of God, He knew these stories would not only be heard by those who were present and heard His words with their own ears. He also knew that they would be spread by "word of mouth" to many others and that they would even eventually be written down for generations to come to learn from, as well.

Oh, what a Savior.

Oh, what a Master Storyteller.

Oh, what a loving God we serve.

STORY ELEVEN

"Stumbling Eyes and Hands"

"If your right eye makes you stumble, tear it out and throw it from you; for it is better for you to lose one of the parts of your body, than for your whole body to be thrown into hell... If your right hand makes you stumble, cut it off and throw it from you; for it is better for you to lose one of the parts of your body, than for your whole body to go into hell." [Matthew 5:29-30]

ZOOMING IN

Next up, in this lovely bunch of coconuts...I mean parables...are two verses that on many lists, are counted as two separate parables (one deals with the eyes and one with the hands). But for the sake of our discussion, here, I felt they were so similar with regards to the message they were conveying, I felt comfortable lumping them together for effect, just as Jesus did.

These two statements, from our Lord, have always been troubling for many people, especially men, because if we were to take them literally, there would be a lot more men walking around with one eye or one hand, instead of two (or maybe none, for the frequent offenders, I would be eyeless and handless, I am sure, by now). And what do you do if you mess up more than four times (two eyes and two hands)? I do not even want to think about it, how about you?

I can only imagine what the Disciples must have been thinking, probably subtly glancing at each other, wondering if He was telling them to do what they thought He was telling them to do. And the people below, down on the hillside, they were probably thinking, "Might be time to pack up and head for the parking lot to try to beat the traffic." I am sure they didn't want to think about how this might apply to them, personally. Plus, they were likely there with their wives and family. So, if they let on that they were troubled by what the Master Storyteller was saying to them, it would be a big-time admission of guilt. I can almost hear them saying, "C'mon, let's go. I've heard enough!!"

But, the interesting thing about what Jesus is actually saying here, is that if they had "ears to hear" and "eyes to see" (spiritually), they would have understood that it is not our eyes or our hands that cause us to sin, it's our hearts. Temptation starts down deep, in the very core of our beings. If we allow it to fester, it then inflames the mind by cranking up our "pleasure centers." Then, if we don't pull the plug on it there, signals get sent to the other parts of the body, the eyes, the hands, whatever...and they simply respond to the impulse that came from the brain and originated in the heart, in the first place.

James, the half-brother of Jesus explained it this way, *"But each one is tempted when he is carried away and enticed (in his heart) by his own lust. Then when lust has conceived (in the brain), it gives birth to sin (in the body); and when sin is accomplished, it brings forth death." [James 1:14-15]*

So, if anyone actually did pluck out an eye or cut off a hand, it was really a sign that they truly did not understand the moral of these stories. And like I have said before, one of the main reasons that Jesus often spoke in parables was to separate the sheep from the goats, to reveal those who were with Him and those who were not.

This was a mighty extreme example of it, though. There were probably some who thought He might be endorsing bodily mutilation, for religious reasons (which of course, He was not). I'm sure many times, when Jesus spoke, He was greatly misunderstood by those who heard Him. And when they later relayed what they thought they heard to others, I am sure many times, it got twisted even further. So, you can imagine, no doubt, how this story might have gotten blown out of proportion by the time it was retold a dozen times or so.

But, we should never underestimate the power of temptation, or the craftiness of our deceiver. He, indeed, is a roaring lion, roaming around constantly, seeking those that he may devour. But in Christ, we do have the power to resist him. Thank you, Lord.

ZOOMING OUT

As we saw in the two earlier parables from this famous sermon, the one about salt and the one about the city set on a hill, Jesus was addressing "mounting questions" that had been cropping up in the minds of not just the common folk, but the religious and political leaders of the day, as well. But, He was not going to soften His message, so as to not make waves. No, that was not our Lord. He was sent here, by the Father, specifically to make waves and to challenge all the false pretenses and concepts that had developed over the many years of man's involvement. They were constantly tinkering with the things of God. Jesus Christ came precisely for that reason, to reset the table (or overturn them, if need be). At this point, He was not worried about ruffling feathers or hurting peoples' feelings. He was more interested in shocking them into taking another look at the things that truly matter. Some were drawn by His words, which were welcomed, while others were repelled.

I have often used the illustration that, when we are faced with something that shakes us to the core or something happens that overwhelms us to the point of questioning what we truly believe, like a tragic death of a loved one or a horrific tragedy in the news, one of two things usually happens. It will draw you closer to God or cause you to withdraw further from Him. It is like when during a game of billiards, you shoot the cue ball towards an object ball. When the impact comes (the shocking event), it causes the object ball to be rapidly moved in one direction or the other. It is the same way with these life events that take us by surprise or cause us to reevaluate. They are likely to push us one way or the other, towards God or away from Him. And the choice, of course, is ultimately ours.

You see, our entire life is like a really long billiards game. One impacting event after another. Each shot has the potential to move us towards victory or further towards defeat. But there is really nothing random about it; we are the shooter. We are the one holding the cue stick and lining up the shot. We determine which way the object ball will go, not our opponent. Although, he will try to push us in the other direction, if we will let him.

I'm just truly thankful and pleased that I understood the parable was not really about eyes or hands. It would be really hard to shoot pool with one hand or with one eye, or type this book, for that matter.

We serve a loving and gracious God. He always is for our good, and never out to harm us. So, when the storms of life blow on us, we need to pause and ask for His help in lining up the next shot. Each shot moves us towards the next one. So, if you play the first one properly, you will be in much better position for successfully making the following shot. And it takes many successful shots for us to end up, ultimately, where God would desire us to be. But we can only take it one shot at a time, one decision at a time. And if we ask for His help, at every juncture along the way, He will lead us to victory, eventually. Even if it does not look or feel like it, at the precise moment.

STORY TWELVE

"The Blind Leading the Blind"

And He also spoke a parable to them: "A blind man cannot guide a blind man, can he? Will they not both fall into a pit? A pupil is not above his teacher; but everyone, after he has been fully trained, will be like his teacher. Why do you look at the speck that is in your brother's eye, but do not notice the log that is in your own eye? Or how can you say to your brother, 'Brother, let me take out the speck that is in your eye,' when you yourself do not see the log that is in your own eye? You hypocrite, first take the log out of your own eye, and then you will see clearly to take out the speck that is in your brother's eye." [Luke 6:39-42]

ZOOMING IN

For the first time in this book, I am introducing Brother Luke, the physician, into our discussion. I am using his version of The Sermon on the Mount for this chapter, because it includes something pretty important, I think, something that Matthew's version leaves out. Going back to the synergy of the parables, as I have been pointing to, this is another great example of how Jesus would often string these stories together, for effect. So often, the parables are treated as unique and separate stories of wisdom. That is certainly true, as well, to some degree. Each of them do stand on their own, no doubt. But, as we saw in the last chapter and again in this one, the Master Storyteller liked to stitch them together, at times, to make sure the message would sink in. It reminds me of

Philippians 4:4 where Paul writes, **"Rejoice in the Lord always, and again I say rejoice."** Repetition. It works. It is why we are taught to memorize Scripture or meditate on it, by repeating it, over and over again, to make it stick!!

In this chapter, I want to talk about this idea of whether, or not, a blind person should be serving as a guide. Now, I am sure Jesus meant no disrespect to someone without sight and neither do I. Nowadays, if you even hint at the possibility that a person with a handicap of one sort or another might find it hard to do what others without that handicap can do, you could get branded as insensitive in our modern, politically-correct society. Let's not even go there. That is miles away from the point Jesus was making here.

If we just take the suggestion of a blind guide at face value, most of us would say, "Well, obviously, if you need to be led somewhere that requires eyesight to find, a person without the ability to see may not be the best choice." That seems to be a reasonable observation, one that would not sound too harsh or uncaring to most folks. It seems to be logical and practical, in fact. If you showed up for one of those Grand Canyon mule trips that wind their way down into the bottom of the canyon on very narrow, rocky paths that often hug sharp cliffs at considerable heights, only to learn that your mule was blind, would you be rude to insist on a different mule, one that can see? My guess is no one would blame you for being uncomfortable with a blind mule, in that situation. When your own life, or the life of a loved one is hanging in the balance, who could blame you?

That is why I felt looking at Luke's version was so important. Matthew's gospel does not deal with this point and I think the clarity of the story that follows is greatly enhanced by the first part. I do not think, for a second, that Jesus just got on a bit of a roll and started adlibbing. No, I'm sure there was a reason why He chose to give them two for the price of one, here. I have no doubt about that.

So, let's go ahead and talk about the second part, now that we have fully considered the first part and how blindness could be a real problem in some situations.

This time, He is not talking about someone who is blind; He is talking about a person who notices a speck in someone else's eye, while not being able to see the log in their own eye. It is a very vivid picture He is painting, even though it is not one that would be likely happen (referring to someone having a real log in their eye, of course). Yet, this is the illustration that Jesus chooses to use at this point. Do you sense that tinge of sarcasm there? I love it. Jesus can be a bit of a "mocker" at times, and He might exaggerate just a little bit, for the sake of a great story. It reminds me a little bit of when He turned over the tables of the moneychangers in the Temple courtyard. They said He was "angry, yet did not sin." And I believe that. So, I am going to assume a similar thing may have happened here; He "mocked them, but did not sin." OK, I am joking a bit here, but you get my drift. A little sarcasm or exaggeration, at times, helps to get the greater point across.

It is also interesting to note, that while the first part of this grouping deals with a person with little or no ability to see, the second part speaks of someone with good eyesight, good enough to see a speck in someone else's eye. What a contrast. Sometimes having too much of something can be just as bad as not having enough, right? I love how our Lord shows both sides of the coin here. Too often, we only see one side of things and treat it as the whole coin or the whole situation, and we wonder why we end up with misunderstandings or hard feelings. I believe that is exactly why Jesus chose to group these two word pictures together. The whole story is often greater than the sum of the parts. This is "synergy" at work.

I would say that the moral of these two stories is also quite similar. You don't want to be led by someone or something that is without good eyesight, where eyesight is critical to the task. And you do not want to be the one offering up advice, or trying to fix someone else's view of things, when your own view is hindered or unreliable. Both sides of that coin will cause you to come up short. I have always been one who enjoys watching a good magician or illusionist at work. Hence, I have always known that what my eyes can see, cannot always be trusted. I think Jesus is saying the same thing. In this case, I think "the log in your own eye" is our sin. It is sin that blinds us to the truth.

Remove the sin, and you will see more clearly. Simple, really.

ZOOMING OUT

When I think of how these two parables, regarding eyesight, play into the bigger picture of our Lord speaking in front of a large gathering on a hillside overlooking the sea and the "mounting questions" that many of these people surely must have had, I cannot help but think that they must have been thinking, "Who is this man, who on one hand gives a blind man back his sight, yet tells us not to be led by a blind man?" This must have been very disconcerting for them. He seemed to be trying to enlighten them by causing them to look at things differently, to be willing to look outside of the traditional religious boxes they grew up in. But at the same time, He was challenging core values and perceptions that they had embraced their entire lives. Were they, now, to just throw it all away, like a rotten apple?

This was a group of people who had very high regard for the traditions of their fathers and grandfathers. To now be told they needed to look beyond tradition and embrace something new and completely different, this was a difficult pill to swallow, even if it was true. They certainly did not want to disrespect their own fathers. But at the same time, what if their fathers were wrong? Should they continue down the same path, one that leads to death and eternal separation from God, just because that is how their ancestors believed?

One thing that a Master Storyteller knows how to do is "strike a nerve." He or she should know quite well how to provoke a reaction, whether a good one or a bad one. After all, it is not really a good story if it does not have a lasting effect on those who hear or read it. I would say that for these stories to continue to be written and talked about for a little over two thousand years, that's a pretty good amount of time, long enough to be considered a "lasting effect."

Jesus Christ did not speak to entertain. He spoke to affect change in the hearts and minds of the listeners. As the Scriptures tell us, *"So will My word be which goes forth from My mouth; It will not return to Me empty, without accomplishing what I desire." [Isaiah 55:11]*

He was, Himself, the Living Word of God, the Word that became flesh and dwelt among us. He had every intention of accomplishing all that the Father had sent Him to do.

STORY THIRTEEN

"Don't Worry, Be Happy"

"For this reason, I say to you, do not be worried about your life, as to what you will eat or what you will drink; nor for your body, as to what you will put on. Is not life more than food, and the body more than clothing? Look at the birds of the air, that they do not sow, nor reap nor gather into barns, and yet your heavenly Father feeds them. Are you not worth much more than they? And who of you by being worried can add a single hour to his life? And why are you worried about clothing? Observe how the lilies of the field grow; they do not toil nor do they spin, yet I say to you that not even Solomon in all his glory clothed himself like one of these. But if God so clothes the grass of the field, which is alive today and tomorrow is thrown into the furnace, will He not much more clothe you? You of little faith!" [Matthew 6:25-30]

ZOOMING IN

There is something about those two little words "do not," that immediately cause many of us to recoil a little bit. It's like, "Uh-oh, brace yourself. Here it comes." I have often thought that if Matthew had maybe just combined the two words and changed one little letter, making "do not" into "donut" it would have been a lot easier to swallow. But, maybe that is just me. My father used to say, "If you want somebody to do something, just tell them not to." Works every time. Those of us who are parents can relate, I'm sure.

Nevertheless, Jesus starts off this beautiful parable with those two little words, right up front. It is one of the chuckholes on the road to sanctification for most Christians. Do not fear. Do not be anxious. Do not worry. Do not judge. Do not be angry. How are you doing with all these golden nuggets of wisdom? Me, not so well. Oh, I try. But, I worry about giving into fear and so I become anxious, or sometimes, even angry. But don't judge me, okay?

Seriously though, I am sure we all would agree that it is hard to quit smoking or drinking. Problems like that are more obvious and people can see when you fail to follow through. But, I would say overcoming anxiety or fear is every bit as hard. Wouldn't you? Maybe someday they will come up with an anxiety patch or a pill that lessens our urge to be fearful. They would sell millions, no doubt. I can see it now, commercials for "Couragra" (to give you courage) or "Anxietra" (to lessen your anxiety). I wonder what the side effects of these drugs might be. They should not cause rapid heart rate or suicidal thoughts, since that is part of what they would be trying to control, right?

"Is not life more than food, and the body more than clothing?"

This is my favorite part of this entire parable. I thought it is interesting that the first part of this statement was targeted more at the men and the second part, more towards the women (or am I reading something into it there?). You must admit, though, how much time to we spend worrying about what we are going to eat (and when) or what clothes to wear, even to church (which by itself seems a little strange to me since God looks at the heart, not our shoes or our hair or the lack thereof, in my case).

I think part of the problem, at least for me, is fully grasping the idea that what matters most is how God sees us, not what other men or women think. Oh sure, we say we don't really care about what other people think of us, but our actions tell a different story. One of my favorite men of the Bible was John the Baptist. Now there was a person who really did not care much about how people viewed him. Matthew writes, ***"John's clothes were made of camel hair, and he had a leather belt wrapped around his waist. His food was locusts and wild honey."*** But people flocked to him anyway, to hear his message and be baptized by him. He was the one chosen by God to prepare the way for His Son, Jesus, the

Savior of the World. Certainly, he could have dressed up a little bit, right? All he was concerned with was obeying God, preparing the way for the One who had long been promised. His message was one of repentance. Outer appearance had nothing to do with it.

I think that if we could fully grasp one little verse, eight little words from Psalm 46, ***"Be still and know that I am God,"*** we would be miles ahead towards finding that peace and tranquility that God promises us. The New American Standard version doesn't say "Be still" it says, "Cease striving." For me that hits the nail more squarely on the head. Sometimes I think my middle name is, Striver, Robert Striver Palumbo. Hmmm, it has a certain ring to it, does it not?

Help me, Lord, to learn to be still, to cease from striving to do things on my own as if I might be bothering You, Lord, if I were to ask for Your help. Amen.

ZOOMING OUT

So where might this simple, yet beautiful story fit into the bigger picture of things? I have dubbed the second discourse, or grouping for this book called The Sermon on the Mount, as dealing with a series of "mounting questions." Well, I think it is no stretch to imagine that almost everyone gathered on that hillside that day was feeling a bit anxious, some maybe fearful and more than a few might even have become angry with what they were hearing.

Here is this newcomer, someone who most of these folks knew very little about, telling them to relax. He's suggesting that they be more like the birds or the grass, in other words, "Don't worry about your clothes, you are beautiful just the way God made you. As for food, just trust that God will provide that, as well. Sure, easy for Him to say. "Should I just quit my job then, lie around in my pajamas all day and just wait for God's food truck to pull up to the door, three times a day? How silly is this guy? He has no idea what my life is like. I wish it were that easy."

To some, I am sure they felt like Jesus was talking down to them. But, that was nothing new. Remember back in John Chapter Two, when He said the Temple would be destroyed and He would raise it back up in three days? Do you think there was some skepticism and anxiety, even anger, about that claim on the part of those who heard it, first hand? I would say, "No doubt."

The words of Jesus Christ were not always perceived as gentle, loving or compassionate. But that was because, so many times, the hearers did not know or realize who was actually speaking to them, God Himself. God is love. He is not just loving or one who exudes love. He is love. He is made of 100% pure love, a love that is purer than anything we will ever encounter in this world, that's for sure.

Even when He seemed harsh or abrupt, His motivation was love, redemption and restoring what was lost in the Garden of Eden. But most did not see it. They took what they heard at face value and considered how it would affect their everyday lives...food, money, clothes, reputation or even sex. It was all about the "here and now". Jesus was all about the "hereafter." The answers to their "mounting questions" required them to take a much longer view of things, far beyond the tips of their noses.

Sound familiar? If so, I believe you are right. Not much has changed in two thousand years. We just need to remember, as I talked about in my first book, "Unlocking Creation," fear and faith are polar opposites and there really is no middle ground. If you are not acting out of one, you are acting out of the other. It is a really good "rule of thumb." Say to yourself, *"Am I making this decision (whatever it is) based on faith and God's Word? If I am not, I am acting out of fear."* That might sound like an oversimplification, but, it really is the truth. If it's not one, it's the other. Period.

STORY FOURTEEN

"GOOD, GOOD FATHER"

"Or what man is there among you who, when his son asks for a loaf, will give him a stone? Or if he asks for a fish, he will not give him a snake, will he? If you then, being evil, know how to give good gifts to your children, how much more will your Father who is in heaven give what is good to those who ask Him!" [Matthew 7:9-11]

ZOOMING IN

What do you know, here we are right back on food, again? Some of you may be thinking, "Okay, I know what this guy battles with." Well, yes, it is true. I do love my food; after all, I am Italian. But, no, it is not one of my biggest struggles. I have bigger ones, trust me. But let's save those for another book. I'd rather stick to the subject, for now. Thank you.

Just as with the words "do not" which we discussed at length in the last chapter, the word "father" is another one of those "trigger words." It tends to stir up reactions, almost immediately, inside of our bodies, hearts and minds. For some of us, it is a word that brings good memories and causes us to reflect on the valuable lessons we learned growing up. They are lessons that have served us well in our adult years.

Thanks be to God, I am among those who have good feelings generated whenever the word "father" is uttered. My father was a great man. Not perfect, to be sure, but a very good man, for the most part. He was physically strong, tough, good-looking and he had a great sense of humor. But maybe the greatest trait that my Dad possessed, at least in my mind, was his role as "the protector." You never wanted to be perceived by my Dad as being a threat to his wife, his children, his friends or his property. That would not end well for you. Take my word on that. Many people discovered that about my Dad the hard way. They usually did not make that mistake twice.

I could probably fill up the rest of this book with real life examples of that and some of them were quite entertaining, to say the least, but I will spare you the details. And like I said, I am struggling to stick to the topic here. So, pardon me, if you will, I have been known to wander off subject at times. But you probably have already noticed that. Alrighty then, where were we?

Oh yes, fathers. Of course, not everyone has a wealth of good memories and feelings whenever the subject of fathers comes up. I had numerous friends whose fathers had problems with alcohol, gambling, womanizing or had been in jail at some point. Some of my friends, and friends of our family, had to deal with physically abusive fathers. And sometimes this went on for years, because back then folks were less likely to report it. You just kept your mouth shut and dealt with it, because even if your Dad had problems, he was still your father and it was frowned upon to be disrespectful to him, no matter what.

That may be one thing that has changed for the better in recent years. At least now, if there is physical abuse going on, either against the wife or the children, we are encouraged to report it. There should be "zero tolerance" when it comes to physical abuse within the family. And I think, nowadays, most people would strongly agree and that is good.

But the parable that Jesus is sharing here, is pointing to another type of Father, our Heavenly Father who just so happens to actually be His own Father. As we have talked about before, God is love, totally and completely. There is no darkness in Him at all. He is totally incapable of giving His children anything, but good things. Now that might come as a surprise to some, because the Bible says, "Nothing is impossible with God." Of course, if God Almighty wanted to give something bad to His children, He could. It is not physically impossible for Him. But, it is not His nature to do so, because He is "love perfected." So, it is His divine nature that would stop Him from giving bad things to His children, not that He physically was unable to do so. I hope that clears this up a little. He is God. He is good. In Him, there is only light, for He is the light of the world.

This parable is primarily about prayer. It is about making our requests known to God. Seek and you will find. Ask and it shall be given to you. No matter what you are dealing with in your life, ask God to be involved, ask for His help. Don't ever think you are bothering Him (as I mentioned in the last chapter) or think that your problems are too small for the God of the Universe to be concerned with.

They are not. As the Chris Tomlin song says, He is a "Good, Good Father." I love that song. We play it on our worship team quite frequently. And it always causes me to reflect on my Heavenly Father, true, but also on my earthly father who I miss dearly. I was so blessed to have him as a positive example. It makes it so much easier to approach my Heavenly Father with confidence. There are so many people who struggle with that because their earthly father was not approachable or even good to them.

Lord, I pray for those folks who struggle with the concept of a God who is a Heavenly Father, a good, good Father, because they had such a poor earthly example to compare it with. May You grant them the grace to forgive and move beyond the negative examples in their past and into Your loving arms. Amen.

ZOOMING OUT

Trying to fit this piece into the puzzle is a little bit easier, actually, than some of the others we've talked about, because at least, it is about something tangible, something we understand, something we have interacted with our whole lives, in one way or the other. A father.

The problem for the people hearing this parable first hand was they had not really looked at God before within the framework of a family relationship. Yes, they knew that one day God would send a Redeemer, a Messiah, but they were not expecting someone to show up one day and proclaim that He is God's Son. This was a whole new ballgame for these folks. The Old Testament prophets did not really foretell of a Son arriving to save them. They were looking forward to a Deliverer, yes, but not necessarily a family member.

Then, if you add to the confusion, the fact that the Son was referring to Himself not only as a Son, but also referring to Himself as the Messiah (as He told the woman at the well) and claiming to be God in the flesh, heads were spinning, I am sure. Can you even imagine what you might have been thinking, if you were among the folks who had grown up in Israel, among those raised under the teachings of the Rabbis and High Priests? These were the ones who knew the Pentateuch and the Prophets frontwards, backwards and inside out. Then, mix in that you never heard anyone say that one day God would send His own Son to save His people, and then seemingly out of nowhere, here comes this man claiming to be God's only begotten Son and that you must now follow Him and turn from what you had believed your whole life. That might be a bit conflicting, wouldn't you say?

May I depart from the normal format, here a bit, by saying that this whole subject of a good, good Heavenly Father (now with the addition of a Son arriving on the scene) probably raised more questions than it answered. But as I said before, the words that Jesus spoke, although they were truer than true can be, they did not always clear things up. In some cases, they were not meant to. His words were often a wedge, a two-edged sword, that often cut right down through the middle of things, drawing many towards Him while repelling others away from Him.

He came to separate the sheep from the goats, to find those who were really His, the lost sheep. Interesting thing about lost sheep, they probably want to be found by their shepherd. Unfortunately, not everyone did. And that meant He also had to uncover some folks for what they really were, wolves in sheep's clothing.

At times, I am sure that Jesus felt the remorse of a good, good Father as He had to stand in a very similar place to the father of the Prodigal Son (someone we will talk about at greater length a bit later). But, Jesus was given the assignment of bringing a message of division, in some ways, and peace in other ways. He had to speak the truth in love, knowing some of His little ones would rebel and seek their own way. But it was because of that love, that He had to let them go; knowing, not all of them would find their way back to the fold.

Tough love is real love. Good fathers understand that.

STORY FIFTEEN

"Precious and Few"

"Enter through the narrow gate; for the gate is wide and the way is broad that leads to destruction, and there are many who enter through it. For the gate is small and the way is narrow that leads to life, and there are few who find it. Beware of the false prophets, who come to you in sheep's clothing, but inwardly are ravenous wolves." [Matthew 7:13-15]

Isn't it interesting that right after this short little parable about the straight and narrow way, Jesus instructs those who were listening to beware of wolves in sheep's clothing, meaning the false prophets, and we were just talking about that. The last sentence in the above snippet is not actually part of the parable, itself. But I thought it fit in with the flow here, so I included it. I wasn't thinking, when I mentioned wolves in sheep's clothing (at the end of the last chapter) that the next parable on the list would bring us right back around to these wolves, again. I like to refer those instances as "divine guidance." No, I did not really see this coming, at that point. But God did. I'd like to take credit for the smooth segue, but I cannot. Thank you, Lord.

Many times, when I sit down to write, I have no idea what I am actually going to end up writing. Oh sure, I have a general idea of the topic and how I want to explain it. But, along the way I get inspired by maybe one tidbit or another and that leads to a story, an illustration or whatever hits me at the moment, so I write it down. Then, when I go back and proofread it, it might seem to be more like something that someone else wrote, not me.

I believe that is how the Holy Spirit works in all of us, not just me, if we will only allow ourselves to yield to it. King David expressed the same sentiment when he wrote Psalm 45 to explain his amazement at how God inspired him to write down what was in his heart and share it with others, so we could still be moved by his works centuries later.

He wrote:

My heart overflows with a good theme;
I address my verses to the King;
My tongue is the pen of a ready writer.
[Psalm 45:1]

That is one of the joys of writing for me. I am never quite sure what is going to come out. The Holy Spirit is the One who leads, all we can do is try our best to follow. In fact, the word "inspiration" is derived from "spirit," which comes from the Greek word "pneuma." And pneuma can also be interpreted as "wind" or "breath." So yes, I believe inspiration comes from God, whether it is to write a song, paint a picture or write a book.

And I believe it is also by divine guidance that you have this book in your hands at this moment in time, because as the Bible teaches, all of our days are numbered in advance. Nothing happens purely by chance and God is in control of every tiny detail, whether we choose to acknowledge it or not. So, I would not take it lightly. I believe God has led you to read this book for a reason, and it has nothing to do with me being the author. Trust me on that. God has a much greater goal in mind. His goal is apprehending your heart.

ZOOMING IN

One of the gifts that a truly good storyteller possesses, is the ability to leave you with that one key phrase or one key statement, that stays with you long after the story is over. Jesus most certainly had that ability and used it quite often. Let's look at the first portion of this parable. The part about, of all things, the width of a gate. C'mon now. That could not possibly have any spiritual relevance, could it? I mean, it's just a gate.

Well Jesus said, regarding the gate that leads to life (meaning eternal life), *"...there are few who find it."* Uh-oh. Wait a minute. Is He talking about me? Where is the cut-off? How do I know if I am in, or I am out? Thousands of people were gathered on this hillside, listening to what started out as a somewhat inspiring message. You know the opening part of this sermon well, no doubt.

"Blessed are the pure in heart, for they shall see God."

"Blessed are those who mourn, for they shall be comforted."

"Blessed are the peacemakers, for they shall be called sons of God."

This is all generally positive and uplifting stuff. I am sure most of the folks were feeling pretty good about themselves for a while there, and why not? Jesus was sharing a message of hope, mercy and redemption.

But not long after that, reality sets in as the same teacher who was shining light into their hearts only minutes before, now seemed to be "raining on their parade." And long after they left and headed for home, they probably forgot all about the warm and fuzzy parts, and were left with just this nagging image of a narrow gate that only a few would be able to find. What does it all mean?

It seems this tiny story, about a narrow gate, near the end of a lengthy sermon on a hillside near Jerusalem over two thousand years ago has become, not only for those who were present, but for you and I and all who read the gospels, a matter to be wrestled with. Certainly, not ignored. Is that what they mean when they say a story is a "cliffhanger?" I'd say so. This one certainly left some people hanging.

It seems Jesus is pointing to holiness and purity of heart, as the way to enter the narrow gate, if I am reading this correctly. But at the same time, isn't Jesus the One Who would eventually die for the sins of the world, offering forgiveness to each and every one of us? That sounds more like the wide gate to me. If everyone is forgiven, wouldn't you need a very wide gate?

And right back around to "the kicker" we come. No, you only need a gate wide enough for those who "find it." Remember, not all lost "sheeple" want to be found. Some are quite happy being lost, I presume, rather than being herded around by some shepherd. Some like to "come and go and do as they please." They do not see any real benefit to being controlled or fenced in. Plus, they fail to recognize the dangers of not being protected from their natural enemies. Their focus is only on the "here and now" and finding the best grass to eat. And that makes them easy prey, not being aware of their surroundings and the dangers that lurk about, be they physical dangers or spiritual ones.

Hence, we have the need for a shepherd, hopefully a good one. And when it comes to gates, the narrow one, especially, few are those who find it. But, those who do, they are precious in His sight.

ZOOMING OUT

Sometimes questions only lead to more questions, especially when it comes to matters of faith and God, including the proper way to interact with Him. I sometimes wish that, in this day and age, we had the ability to gather on a hillside and listen to Jesus face-to-face. I would think that would make it all much easier to digest, wouldn't you? But, it doesn't seem that was the case for those who were right there with Him. Sadly, for many, it only led to more confusion and created more frustration. It seems that maybe they were looking for the answers they wanted to hear. But, the Lord had no intention of tickling ears. No, He never took the Dale Carnegie course on "How to Win Friends and Influence People."

Rather, He only spoke the things He had heard His Father say and He only did the things He saw His Father do. He was not interested in compromising His message to lure people in His direction and His intent was not to destroy the traditions of the Jewish faith, as some surmised He was intent on doing. After all, He said He came to fulfill the Law, not abolish it.

His only goal was to reunite fallen people with the One who made them, by simply speaking the truth in love. He wanted them to focus more on what was ahead, than on what was behind them. Jesus knew that people cannot change their past, but they can most certainly change their future. He also knew they would never change if they were content to follow the masses, go with what's popular or become too comfortable with the old cloth or the old wine that we talked about earlier. The "mounting question" being raised by this parable was about holiness, sanctification and being willing to leave the old ways behind and embracing the new.

Jesus Christ introduced the world to an entirely new way of "being holy." In days gone by, it was believed you were holy only if you followed the Laws of Moses perfectly and completely. But, knowing we all fell short of that, the priest would offer up a sacrificial lamb, once a year, for himself and the sins of all the people. Sure, it was ritualistic, but it seemed to suffice. The people understood it.

Jesus became that Lamb, once and for all time. The yearly offering no longer needed to be made. And being holy was no longer about obeying all the religious laws (which was humanly impossible). Holy meant "being separate, set apart for God." It meant turning from your old life, from following the crowd or trying to earn your own salvation. It meant fully putting your trust in Christ and the blood that was shed as full payment for all the sins of mankind-past, present and future. Being holy now meant accepting God's mercy and turning from the powers of sin and self and submitting to the Holy Spirit. It meant, as they say, to "Let go and let God."

The answer to all these "mounting questions" was Jesus Christ.

He, alone, is "the gate" by which we all must enter through, as He taught us in John, Chapter Ten, nothing more and nothing less.

STORY SIXTEEN

"Two Foundations"

"Therefore, everyone who hears these words of Mine and acts on them, may be compared to a wise man who built his house on the rock. And the rain fell, and the floods came, and the winds blew and slammed against that house; and yet it did not fall, for it had been founded on the rock. Everyone who hears these words of Mine and does not act on them, will be like a foolish man who built his house on the sand. The rain fell, and the floods came, and the winds blew and slammed against that house; and it fell—and great was its fall." [Matthew 7:24-27]

ZOOMING IN

At last, here at the end of Part Two, finally a parable that addresses a subject I have some first-hand experience with (construction and the importance of having a solid foundation). For twenty-two years of my life, I worked as an ironworker. They are the men who put up the steel for buildings and bridges and install reinforcing steel for strengthening concrete structures. When you are erecting a large building or a bridge, you better be very sure that the foundation is deep enough, large enough and solid enough that it will not be affected by weather, seasonal changes or hopefully, even a natural disaster. If not, the building or bridge will likely not stand for very long.

But, I would like to tell you a more personal story, one that occurred during the beginning stages of building our own home in 1991. My wife and I had purchased a lot in a subdivision, the very last lot they had, actually. We had planned on building a house with a basement under half of the house, not the whole house. But on the first day of excavation, I was informed that I would need to do a full basement, because the lot that I had bought was what they called a "fill lot." They had used it as a dump lot for that entire development.

So, the excavators needed to dig down eight feet under the whole house, anyway, to get to "virgin soil" that was solid enough for the foundation to sit on. Suddenly, this parable became very real to me, you might say. There was now a "cost factor" hitting me right between the eyes, just as we were beginning to build our dream house. You can imagine, I'm sure, how upsetting this was to my wife and I, at that point. We had done our due diligence (or so we thought) and had planned well to make sure we could afford to finish the project. And then this pops up on day one. OUCH!!

Jesus said in this parable, ***"Everyone who hears these words of mine and acts on them, may be compared to a wise man who built his house on the rock."*** I certainly wish I had consulted with a wise man who knew something about what is or what is not a "buildable lot" before we broke ground. It would have saved a lot of anguish later. It was a lesson learned.

So, the point of this parable which was the final one, the closing statements of His famous Sermon on the Mount, was to not only give those "with ears to hear" some sound advice that could greatly impact their daily lives, which was what this sermon was primarily about, but to also drive home the point that, if they were wise, they would not just hear His advice, but apply it. For if they did not, there would surely be consequences down the road, when the storms of life raged against them. We all can attest to the fact that those storms will come, no matter who you are or how much money you make, the winds of life will blow. So, you better have that solid foundation, that firm footing to withstand them. This was just some real solid and practical advice Jesus was sharing on that day. But, some could not receive it because they were so distracted by the One who was doing the talking. Sound familiar?

ZOOMING OUT

Here we are, eight parables and eight mounting questions later, and many eyes still could not see and many ears still could not hear. These questions were being answered, clearly enough, by the One who was sent from above to do just that, but they just could not seem to grasp it. It was new wine and tasted a little bitter to them. Besides, they liked the old wine. Why change?

So many were getting bogged down in the details. "Why are we talking about salt?" "What is all this chatter about plucking out an eye or chopping off a hand?" "I know I'm not supposed to be anxious or fearful, but I have bills to pay, crops to plant, children to raise. Does this man not understand the struggles of life we all deal with?" "Of course, God is a good Father. I never doubted that." "I pray all the time. Why are my prayers not answered? Does He not hear us?" "And why is a narrow gate better than a wide one? I always thought bigger was better." "Now, He wants to tell me how to build my house. Who doesn't know that a firm foundation is better than building on sinking sand?"

I can just hear all the rumblings coming from the people as they headed back to their homes or mingled in the marketplace. "Who was this man, who thinks He has all the answers? I have a good head on my shoulders. I don't need Him to tell me how to live." "No wonder the priests and politicians are so upset with Him. He is just a troublemaker."

And even as I read over these statements, I can't help but think that the very same things might be said, right here and right now, if Jesus were to show up (or someone claiming to be Jesus, because remember, these folks were not convinced He was who He claimed to be) and went on television in front of millions of people and started telling people that everything they believed their whole lives was wrong. Saying they could not earn salvation by being good or through their own efforts, but only by putting their complete trust and faith in Him and Him alone. He might be lucky just to get off out of there alive, I presume, especially if there was a large audience like maybe in a big theater or a stadium, which might be the case nowadays.

You know how they like to promote these great big live events, like sports, concerts or major political happenings like a Presidential election or an Inauguration Ceremony. Big bucks can be made by selling commercial time for such a high profile happening. The networks wouldn't want to miss out on a "live event" featuring the return of Jesus Christ, sharing a long-awaited message intended for the whole world to hear. Talk about "Must

See TV" (provided, of course, it was really Jesus and not one of those wolves in sheep's clothing).

And therein lies the rub, not only for us today, but for those back then. How could you know for sure? What proof would you require? And even if you did ask for proof, would the returning King feel the need to provide it?

Or would He simply ask us to have faith, believe, to put our trust in Him as He did two thousand years ago? Would that be good enough for you? Or me?

One day we are going to find out. He is coming again. He said it and I believe it. But will the world accept Him when He comes this time around?

Are you ready to accept Him now, based on the words He gave us back then? Do you believe He was who He said He was, in your heart? Or do you need more proof?

When Jesus had finished these words, the crowds were amazed at His teaching; for He was teaching them as one having authority, and not as their scribes. [Matthew 7:28-29]

PART THREE

"Kingdom Answers"

"The kingdom of heaven is like..."

Matthew 13:44

STORY SEVENTEEN

"A Story About Reaping"

"That day Jesus went out of the house and was sitting by the sea. And large crowds gathered to Him, so He got into a boat and sat down, and the whole crowd was standing on the beach."
[Matthew 13:1-2]

We now move into the third cluster of parables, or "bunch of carrots," as we have been calling them in this book with a tip of the hat to my friend's daughter, of course. We have just finished the second bunch, from the "Sermon on the Mount", and now we come to this bunch, that I like to refer to as the "Sermon from the Boat."

Matthew tells us that Jesus came out of a house, overlooking the Sea of Galilee in Capernaum, and finds a large group of people gathered there, much like a celebrity would find the paparazzi outside of their house nowadays. So, He climbs into a boat, to give Himself some space from the crowd, I presume, and sits down and begins to preach. He then proceeds to rattle off seven incredible stories, or parables (some with explanations, some without). But they all have a similar theme, the Kingdom of Heaven.

Let's have a look, shall we? First up, one of the most famous parables of all, the Parable of the Sower.

And He spoke many things to them in parables, saying, "Behold, the sower went out to sow; and as he sowed, some seeds fell beside the road, and the birds came and ate them up. Others

fell on the rocky places, where they did not have much soil; and immediately they sprang up, because they had no depth of soil. But when the sun had risen, they were scorched; and because they had no root, they withered away. Others fell among the thorns, and the thorns came up and choked them out. And others fell on the good soil and yielded a crop, some a hundredfold, some sixty, and some thirty. He who has ears, let him hear."
[Matthew 13:3-9]

ZOOMING IN

Here we have the Lord talking about birds, again. A few chapters back, He was complimenting them because they did not worry about what to eat, trusting God to provide for them. Here, we find out they were eating seeds that were not meant for them to eat. So, maybe not all the birds were walking (or flying) by faith. Maybe some of them were grabbing whatever they could get, whenever they could get it, not unlike many of us. But, of course, that is not the lesson the Master Storyteller wanted His listeners to focus on, here.

This story was much more about the quality of soil you may be investing time and effort into, to some degree, trying to produce a future harvest of some kind. And for the one doing the sowing in this story, the results of his labor will undoubtedly affect not only the sower, himself, but his family and others, as well. It is rare that our efforts only yield results that just affect us, the one doing the planting. It almost always affects others, in fact many times, that is why we are planting in the first place, to benefit others, not just ourselves. Isn't that an illustration we could apply to all the many blessings of God? They were never intended to be just for us, alone. They were intended to be shared with others, just as He shares His great bounty and wisdom with us, right?

We see the Lord putting a ton of emphasis here on the quality of the soil and I believe that is very important. That is why farmers generally rotate their crops from one field to another every so often. The soil, sometimes, gets depleted of nutrients and needs to have time to be replenished and to rest to give it a chance to rejuvenate and be ready to yield a bountiful crop once again (that might be another lesson hidden in this parable, the importance of times of resting and rejuvenation). But, Jesus seems to be focusing in on why the soil may be good or bad. Is it rocky? How deep were the seeds planted? Was the soil covered with weeds? They all play a role; I have no doubt.

While I could probably go on and on about all the different aspects of farming here, I think most of us get the point the Lord is trying to drive home here. It really is a simple concept. You wouldn't cast your seed on Astroturf or asphalt that has been painted green and expect a great crop. Although, sometimes when we share our faith with others, it feels like we are trying to sow our seeds on hard pavement. It doesn't seem to be able to take root and maybe that is part of what the Master Storyteller is suggesting here. Get to know the soil, before you decide to plant there. Make sure it is fertile ground. If you need to spend some time preparing it first, do so. It makes a huge difference, when soil is properly prepared to receive the seed.

But, I'd like to take a moment to point out one other key aspect of the parables of Jesus Christ and this one is maybe the best example of it. Sometimes, He felt compelled to give an interpretation of His parables (usually to His Disciples), but many times He did not (usually to those who were skeptical of Him). For this one, He gives a long and detailed explanation, one of the best ones of all, really.

Check it out:

"Hear then the parable of the sower. When anyone hears the word of the kingdom and does not understand it, the evil one comes and snatches away what has been sown in his heart. This is the one on whom seed was sown beside the road. The one on whom seed was sown on the rocky places, this is the man who hears the word and immediately receives it with joy; yet he has no firm root in himself, but is only temporary, and when affliction or persecution arises because of the word, immediately he falls away. And the one on whom seed was sown among the thorns, this is the man who hears the word, and the worry of the world and the deceitfulness of wealth choke the word, and it becomes unfruitful. And the one on whom seed was sown on the good soil, this is the man who hears the word and understands it; who

indeed bears fruit and brings forth, some a hundredfold, some sixty, and some thirty." [Matthew 13:18-23]

Now, you understand why I didn't go into too much of an explanation of this parable. If the Master Storyteller was willing to give His own interpretation, what good would it have been for me to go on and on, adding my own take on things. It is far better that you get the answers right from the source, the Living Word of God, Himself.

ZOOMING OUT

And the disciples came and said to Him, "Why do You speak to them in parables?" Jesus answered them, "To you it has been granted to know the mysteries of the kingdom of heaven, but to them it has not been granted. For whoever has, to him more shall be given, and he will have an abundance; but whoever does not have, even what he has shall be taken away from him. Therefore, I speak to them in parables; because while seeing they do not see, and while hearing they do not hear, nor do they understand". [Matthew 13:10-13]

Part Three of this book is entitled, "Kingdom Answers," which seems like a good follow-up to all those "Mounting Questions" we found in Part Two. And right here, in the first parable from this very important bunch, we come across a portion of Scripture so key to what we are discussing, I included it on the Title Page for the book. "To you, these mysteries have been revealed. But to them, not so much." Think about that, for a moment.

So, right up front, Jesus is answering maybe one of the most important questions of all, from the perspective of the Kingdom of Heaven. He basically says, "Not everyone is going to be able to see it or understand it." Okay, I'm a little confused again. If Jesus is going to come to Earth and give His life for the sins of all mankind, wouldn't you think He would speak in such a way that everyone would clearly understand? Wasn't that the reason He came, to reveal truth and open eyes and hearts?

My answer to that would be (and I pray it would line up with His own answer, since I am sort of speaking on His behalf here, somewhat), He could see into their hearts. He knew, even before any of us are born, which ones were going to accept His invitation of mercy, grace and love, and which ones never would, no matter what He said. In Isaiah, we learn that the potter (a symbol of God Almighty) makes one vessel for honor and another for dishonor. Is that possible? Could God have known, for instance, before He made Adolf Hitler or the Boston Strangler, what monsters they would turn out to be. I believe the answer is "Yes," as much as it pains me to say so. Then, doesn't that lead to the question as to why God made them anyway, if He knew they were going to do such terrible things? Again, yes, but remember God knows in advance, we do not.

If He was going to grant humans "free will," He had to let us choose to sin, if that is the choice we desired to make. If He were to step in and stop the bad ones from being born, wouldn't He be "rigging the game in His favor?" It wouldn't truly be "free will" at all, then, would it?

All of us are sinners, right? The same logic could be applied to you and me. If God was going to step in, as the potter, and decide to make only "vessels of honor," would you and I have born in the first place? And if we were born, would we have a full menu of choices to choose from, even the sinful choices?

We might still choose to follow God, at some point, but it would be without all the alternative choices. Would that still truly be "free will?" We must remember, it is the presence of evil, that sometimes causes us to look to God as the alternative to the suffering and pain we see around us. So, if we saw no evil in the world, what would be the impetus for us desiring to change?

I know that is a lot to think about, so I will let you chew on that for a while. But I would like to toss out one more factor for us to think about, related to having a great harvest, be it farming or evangelism, if I may.

Obviously, other things may contribute to having a great harvest...not just the soil. The quality of the seed, the weather, the amount of water (too much or too little can be harmful) and maybe one that you might not have thought about, how much prayer has gone into the planning and sowing. Really? Does prayer matter in farming? I would guess if you asked lots of farmers, most would overwhelmingly say, "Yes."

You see, I believe we can do everything just right, whether we are making wine, playing golf, planting corn or writing a book. But, if you do not commit your ways to the Lord in prayer and ask for His help and His direction, you could still be somewhat successful, at least temporarily. But, you will never realize the kind of "lasting success" you could have had, if the Lord had been involved and directed your steps. The Bible says, *"Unless the Lord builds the house, they labor in vain who build it."* [Psalm 127:1]

We need to look at it all in the light of eternity, I believe, because our time on this planet is maybe only seventy or eighty years, if we are lucky. We can possibly be very successful in this life, for sure. And many are, without even thinking of God or asking for His help. But eternity is a long, long time.

Jesus, then, adds another piece to the puzzle:

"For what does it profit a man to gain the whole world, and forfeit his soul?' [Mark 8:36]

This verse often reminds me of the bumper sticker I once saw on a very fancy sports car. It said, *"He who dies with the most toys, wins."*

"Wins what?" I might ask.

STORY EIGHTEEN

"Right...What's A Tare?"

"The kingdom of heaven may be compared to a man who sowed good seed in his field. But while his men were sleeping, his enemy came and sowed tares among the wheat, and went away. But when the wheat sprouted and bore grain, then the tares became evident also. The slaves of the landowner came and said to him, 'Sir, did you not sow good seed in your field? How then does it have tares?' And he said to them, 'An enemy has done this!' The slaves said to him, 'Do you want us, then, to go and gather them up?' But he said, 'No; for while you are gathering up the tares, you may uproot the wheat with them. Allow both to grow together until the harvest; and in the time of the harvest I will say to the reapers, "First gather up the tares and bind them in bundles to burn them up; but gather the wheat into my barn." [Matthew 13:24-30]

ZOOMING IN

For those of you who may be old enough to remember back to Bill Cosby's early days in comedy (I am guilty as charged here), he was a very funny stand-up comedian. In those days, his humor was "G-rated" as most comedians were back then. I miss those days. Red Skelton, Bob Hope, Bill Cosby, Jonathan Winters. All very funny and very clean.

One of my favorite Cosby bits, from those days, was his take on Noah and the Ark. God calls out to Noah, saying, "Noah, I am going to cover the Earth with a flood. I want you to build an ark, so you and your family can survive along with two of each variety of animal" (I'm paraphrasing from memory, here). God continues, "I want you to build an ark of gopher wood, three hundred cubits, by fifty cubits, by thirty cubits." Noah thinks for a minute and replies, "Right....what's a cubit?" That was a classic. Hence, the name for this chapter, "Right...what's a tare?"

I am calling Part Three, "Kingdom Answers" because the Lord opened six of the seven parables from Matthew 13 with the words, "The kingdom of heaven is like." And I truly believe the first one we looked at here, the "Parable of the Sower" spoke of a Kingdom principle as well, even though Jesus did not actually use those words. It is true that God allows for His seed, His message of love, hope to be spread all over the world to every nation, tribe and tongue, upon good soil and bad. I believe God is able to reveal Himself, and does so, to every man, woman and child who has ever lived or will ever live here on Earth. Some of us would be considered "good soil" because we are accepting of His message and our hearts have been prepared, as good soil is, to give these seeds of life the best chance of bearing fruit. Other folks, for one reason or another are more like rocky soil. The seed does not even sink in...so it is easily eaten by those nasty birds or other varmints (don't you just love that word, "varmints?" I do. (Okay, maybe I watched too many episodes of the Beverly Hillbillies). So yes, the quality of the soil is critical to a good harvest, no doubt.

Now, we move on to another aspect of good farming, especially if you are a grower of wheat, "beware of the tare." Having heard this story told and retold hundreds of times, I have always thought of the word "tares" as meaning weeds. Others have referred to it as the chaff, as in the wheat and the chaff. While those are pretty good explanations and they do seem to help us to get to the heart of the parable, I did a little more digging to see if there is something more specific to be learned about those pesky things called tares.

And what do you know, there is. Easton's Bible Dictionary defines the word tares this way:

It is the Lolium temulentum, a species of rye-grass, the seeds of which are a strong soporific poison. It bears the closest resemblance to wheat till the ear appears, and only then the difference is discovered. It grows plentifully in Syria and Palestine.

So, yes, while tares can be generalized to be understood as weeds or chaff, I believe the Lord was using the word, specifically, to reveal something a little more stealth-like or devious about these "chokers of good seed." Which is not unlike our spiritual enemy, Satan, who is also quite stealth-like and devious in his deceptions.

Turns out, if you buy good seed (which is why they asked the landowner if he sowed good seed into his field), it will not likely have tares mixed in with it, just good quality wheat seed. And that is why the landowner replied, "An enemy has done this." The Lord was saying, "God only sows good seed. It is our enemy who comes and sprinkles in bad seed, with the good, to choke out the good harvest before it has a chance to grow to maturity."

But what makes tares so hard to discover, at least early on, is that it looks exactly like wheat. Until the ear appears, as the definition says, they look exactly alike. But by that time, the damage has been done and some of the good crop may have been lost.

But it is the last part of this story, in my opinion, that is so important to understand and it answers two of the most frequent questions that unbelievers ask concerning God. "Why does God allow bad things to happen to good people." And, "Why does God not punish the bad people sooner?"

The slaves ask the landowner if they should start trying to pick out the tares from among the wheat, now, before the damage is done. He answers them, *"No; for while you are gathering up the tares, you may uproot the wheat with them. Allow both to grow together until the harvest."*

That is because he wanted to wait until the ear appeared, at harvest time. Then, when they harvested it all, they could more easily tell one from the other and destroy the tares without damaging a single grain of wheat. He did not want to risk plucking out the good stuff with the bad.

Thank you, Lord. You or I could have very easily been plucked, collateral damage, while He was trying to take out the bad guys. Rather, God chooses to let them both run their course, for in the end, the differences will be crystal clear and the chaff (tares) will pay the price it deserves to pay, while the wheat or "the good seed" remains unpunished. Hallelujah!!

ZOOMING OUT

I think the "Kingdom Answers" provided by this bunch of stories, and how they apply to the underlying theme of the greater parable that the Master Storyteller is weaving throughout His earthly ministry, should be rather easy to grasp. In the story of the sower, we are taught the importance of good soil, the importance of being "properly prepared to receive" the good seed that God is sowing in us through Jesus Christ.

Now, here in this story, we learn to watch out for the bad seed that the enemy tries to mingle in with the Lord's good seed. The trouble is, many times it looks very similar. The devil is very sly. The apple that Adam and Eve were seduced into eating looked like good fruit that could have been produced from good seed. But it was spiritually poisonous, just as we learned the tares are "soporifically poisonous" to the wheat crop. The bad seed kills off the good seed before we have a chance to identify it as bad seed.

Here is what King Solomon had to say on the subject:

Every man's way is right in his own eyes,
But the Lord weighs the hearts. [Proverbs 21:2]

To us humans, as fallen creatures corrupted by sin, our eyes have even a harder time telling the wheat from the tares, or that which the Lord is sowing into us *versus* that which the enemy is trying to trick us with. They both look pretty good sometimes, right? That is why, especially for us men folk, our eyes are not to be trusted. My eyes really like the way those tares look sometimes, just saying. If I trust my eyes to determine what is good, I could be fooled quite easily. That is why the Lord looks at our hearts. That is where our true motives and agendas lie. Our eyes can be fooled and our ears can be fooled, but if we fill our hearts with His Word, if we eat the daily bread of life and allow it to nourish us and breathe life into the innermost parts of our being, we will not easily be fooled by the subtle tricks of the Deceiver.

Beware of the tares, my friends. Let the light of the Lord reveal them for what they truly are...seeds sown by "an enemy," as the story tells us. This enemy seeks to choke the very life out of anything or anyone that belongs to our Creator.

As it was in the beginning, it is now. Nothing has changed. And it will never change until the Lord comes back and gives "the devil his due," a one-way trip to the Lake of Fire.

STORY NINETEEN

"The Smallest of Seeds"

"The kingdom of heaven is like a mustard seed, which a man took and sowed in his field; and this is smaller than all other seeds, but when it is full grown, it is larger than the garden plants and becomes a tree, so that the birds of the air come and nest in its branches." [Matthew 13:31-32]

ZOOMING IN

So, what do you think? Should the size of a seed matter, if we apply some of the other lessons we learned throughout the Scriptures? King David was the smallest and youngest of the eight sons of Jesse. He should have been disqualified immediately. He was also much, much smaller than Goliath, the Philistine champion, and we know how that turned out. But, okay, David had two equalizers. First of all, he was really good with a slingshot and a smooth stone. And secondly (and most importantly), God was on his side. Need I say more?

The poor widow, in Luke 21, only gave two small, copper coins (a mere pittance compared to what some many of the richer folks gave), but it was considered to be a worthier gift because "it was all she had." The richer folks may have given more, in terms of the amount of money donated, but it was only a small percentage of their riches. So, it was not thought to be as worthy of a gift as the poor widow, because the Lord does not weigh amounts as to how our gifts are measured. Rather, He is looking to the attitude of our hearts, again, just as we learned in the last chapter.

He would prefer us to be among those who only gave a little, if it was all we had, to those who gave a lot, but it cost them little compared to what they possessed.

And maybe the clearest example of all is found in Luke 9, where Jesus, Himself, teaches that it is "the least among you. . ." that shall be considered the greatest. So often, we learn that the physical world is sort of like an upside down cake (ooh, I love those!!) when compared to the spiritual world that the Lord would rather have us walking around in, on a daily basis. Yes, even right now, we do not have to wait until we get to Heaven to start applying these Kingdom principles. The Kingdom of God has come down to us through Jesus Christ and we are empowered to walk in it by His Holy Spirit. If you are born again, as Jesus explained to Nicodemus, you can see the Kingdom of God, right here and right now. Jesus told him, ***"that which is born of the Spirit is Spirit."*** He did not say, "will become Spirit." He said, "is Spirit." He was speaking in the present tense, not future tense.

And when we look at creation, it is plain to see that many of these "Kingdom principles" are already at work in this world. I think the mustard seed is one of the best and clearest examples of that. Don't you? Here we have this tiny little seed, that when it is placed in good soil and the weeds are kept away, can grow to be larger than the other plants in the garden. It says it's even considered to be a tree, one in which the birds can nest. There are those birds again. This time they are not eating the seed, they are being more patient and waiting until the seed grows into a future home. Okay, well, no one said they weren't smart. If they ate up all the seeds, they would never have a home, right?

Couldn't we also apply these "Kingdom principles" to the very stories that the Master Storyteller was telling? Many of these, as we have already seen and discussed, were only one or two verses long. They were not long-winded or of flowery speech meant to entertain or captivate an audience for a considerably amount of time. You know how some people are, once they get in front of an audience, they like to hold onto it as long as they can. I think it is an ego thing, to some extent. It is more pleasing to themselves, than the audience sometimes.

Jesus was not like that at all. Short, sweet and boy, was He ever "to the point." There is another verse I'd like to share, that applies to this very subject, if I may, which also further confirms the whole idea that this parable is conveying. And it comes from our good friend King Solomon, again:

When there are many words, transgression is unavoidable, But he who restrains his lips is wise. [Proverbs 10:19]

No doubt, our Lord and Savior was wiser than wise. He steered clear of that trap. He stayed laser-focused on the truth, the message His Father sent Him to convey. He was certainly not one who spoke, just because they liked to hear themselves talk. But, I have known quite of few people in my life who did. How about you? Have you bumped into one or two of those in your life?

And don't say me. Hey, I'm writing a book here. I'm supposed to elaborate. LOL

ZOOMING OUT

It seems that the way in which this "little story," with potentially a big impact for "those who have the ears to hear," fits into the larger story being told by the Master Storyteller has more to do with the end of the story than the beginning. The "Kingdom Answer" that is revealed here is more about the resulting tree than the seed from which it sprouted. And isn't that often the case, when we talk about spiritual things.

It matters not where we started or where we came from, but where we end up that counts, meaning Heaven of course. We are all seeds, to start with (physically and spiritually). We all need to be planted in good soil, be protected from the weeds and be properly fed and watered, if we are ever to bring forth good fruit. And of course, the more fruit we each produce, the more seeds there are to scatter about. There is a gigantic "domino effect" at work here, even though most of us do not always see that potential.

How many times have we heard the slogan, "Just bring one." In essence, it implies that if each of us during our lifetime (and there are roughly 1.8 billion people who profess to be Christians in the world today), just managed to bring one person to Christ, that would mean another 1.8 billion souls who would escape the consequences of sin and death and receive eternal life. And that is just counting those of us who are alive today. That would be an amazing harvest, to say the least.

But, that is not how this all works, according to God's grace and mercy. If one of us saves just one, that person may save one or more and those may go forth and save one or more...and on and on it goes. There is this chance for exponential growth in all of this, where the one person you lead to Christ could result in dozens, maybe even hundreds or more, eventually calling upon the name of Jesus and entering into His eternal Kingdom, all because of one act of faith, one attempt at sharing the Gospel.

The results could amaze you. You never know unless you try. It all starts with one seed, one little seed that grows into an entire tree, one big enough for birds to nest in. A tree big enough to produce a whole lot of mustard (who is not thankful for that?) and a tree big enough to produce thousands of more seeds that all have the potential to start the ball rolling all over again.

The moral of this little story, I think is...REALIZE YOUR POTENTIAL, in Christ.

Our Lord is not big on the whole "one and done" philosophy.

He is much more about "being fruitful and multiplying."

Amen to that!!!

STORY TWENTY

"The Uttering of Hidden Things"

"The kingdom of heaven is like leaven, which a woman took and hid in three pecks of flour until it was all leavened."
All these things Jesus spoke to the crowds in parables, and He did not speak to them without a parable. This was to fulfill what was spoken through the prophet:
"I will open My mouth in parables;
I will utter things hidden since the foundation of the world."
[Matthew 13:33-35]

ZOOMING IN

Talk about a peculiar little story. If any of the parables could have benefited from an explanation by the Storyteller, Himself, this one surely could have used that, I think. One little sentence, talking about a woman hiding some leaven in three pecks of flour. And this is supposed to be like "the Kingdom of heaven." Raise your hand, if you are a little confused by this one. My hand is up, too.

I'm glad we have been doing the "zooming in" and "zooming out" thing for each parable, because this little gem has two prominent takeaways. Three, actually, once we get to the "big picture" part. So, let me start at the end of the verses pasted above here, and work back towards the beginning this time, if I may. I think it may help us to "zoom in" on what Christ is pointing to here. The actual words of Jesus that make up this parable, the red-

111

letter words if you will, are only one brief sentence long. But it is the verses that follow, for me, that hold the key to understanding it.

And once again, these are purely my observations. I am not a theologian or Bible expert. I am just a man who loves the Lord and I have done my best to walk with Him for the last thirty-eight years. I write based on my experiences and what I have learned from others, great authors, pastors and mentors. I have been greatly blessed to have so many wonderful teachers over the years. I believe God has taught me much through them.

But, I don't claim to have all the answers. None of us really do, if we are honest. All we can do is try our best to add something worthwhile to the pile of opinions and interpretations, and hope and pray that it bears witness with those who hear it or read it, by His grace of course, and that it causes them to draw closer to Him, which is the primary goal of my writing in the first place. To point others to Jesus Christ, like the verse, *"O, taste and see that the Lord is good," [Psalm 34:8].* I am just offering free samples here, just like at the grocery store (it's truly the only reason I go!!).

Others may get something completely different from these side stories that Jesus shared. That is fine with me. I really enjoy getting numerous takes on Scripture. The Word of God is so rich, so full of revelation and truth, we can never truly absorb it all in this life. Honestly, every time I read a chapter or a verse that I haven't seen in a while, I find something fresh and new there. That is what makes the Bible the "neverending story," as we discussed earlier. It never gets boring or stale. If we keep our eyes open, there is always fresh manna, like fresh bread just coming out of the oven. I know, it's my stomach is talking again. But, at least this chapter is about food, right? So, I am staying on topic. . . sort of.

One thing I love about Matthew's gospel, is how he often includes Old Testament references, to add weight to the story of Christ. In this instance, he is talking about how Jesus often spoke to the crowds in parables, by pointing to what Asaph wrote in Psalm 78:2, *"I will open my mouth in parables; I will utter things hidden since the foundation of the world."* Matthew shares this as another confirmation that Jesus is the Promised One, the Messiah they have all been waiting for. Trust me, there were still many people who had their doubts, just as many still do today.

But isn't it interesting that Matthew chooses to go back to a psalm that speaks of parables and things hidden since the foundation of the world. And he does it in the very next verse after sharing this parable about a little bit of yeast and a big lump of dough and how the former will greatly change the latter. Coincidence? I think not.

I believe what our Lord was pointing to symbolically there, was the Good News of redemption that He came down from Heaven to reveal. It may have been hidden for years and it may have started out very small, with just a handful of men and women, but it would eventually change the whole world, for better or worse (just like a marriage). But we will talk about that dynamic a bit later, here.

We should also notice, I think, that this little story comes right after Jesus talked about the tiniest of seeds becoming a tree large enough to be a nesting place for the birds of the field (the mustard seed, of course). The Master Storyteller seems to be on a fixed tangent, here. He's making the same point, driving it home a second time, but showing a different side of it. First, there's a tiny seed that has the potential to become a big, beautiful and quite useful tree. Now, we see tiny grains of yeast or leaven where just a pinch can cause a large lump of dough to rise and become something that it never could have become on its own. Glory to God!

All of this seems quite positive and I believe it was the Lord's intent here, to get us to not look down on anyone or anything because of their size or stature. Remember Joshua's victory at Jericho? Did he overpower them with great numbers? Not hardly, you see, that is where faith comes in. Without faith, it is impossible to please God. But with God and by faith, all things are possible, David believed that. He could never have mustered the courage to go up against Goliath, had he not had the faith to know that God was his equalizer. Goliath never had a chance, as I see it.

Do you believe that? Do you believe that with God's help, you can do the impossible? Faith is defined in the Bible, as *". . . the assurance of things hoped for, the conviction of things not seen."* Are you able to believe in things you have not seen with your own eyes? I hope so. If not, you are missing out on the best part of being a Christian.

A wise man once told me, "Science says, 'Seeing is believing,' but Christianity teaches us that, 'Believing is seeing.' " Where are you going to put your trust? In your eyes, or your heart?

ZOOMING OUT

Before we move on to the next parable, I want to talk a little bit about the fact that "leaven" or "yeast" is not always talked about in Scripture as a good thing. Sometimes it was used to illustrate something to be avoided. Pride. Sin. Lies. Reliance on self. These are all examples of types of "spiritual leaven" that might be undesirable and yes, these are talked about in the Bible, too.

Here is what the Apostle Paul had to say about leaven:

You were running well; who hindered you from obeying the truth? This persuasion did not come from Him who calls you. A little leaven leavens the whole lump of dough. I have confidence in you in the Lord that you will adopt no other view." *[Galatians 5:7-10]*

He, of course, is talking about someone outside of their circle, introducing false doctrines into their thinking that were apparently leading some of the Galatians to return to their legalistic roots.

This was a little leaven, the bad kind, that began to spread through the whole community of believers there. So, you see, leaven can be something positive or something negative. I believe Jesus was using it to illustrate the positive attributes of leaven. Paul was showing its more negative potential.

Maybe the most profound and lasting example we have of the dangers of leaven is the "Feast of Unleavened Bread", as Moses taught in Exodus Chapter 12:

"Now this day will be a memorial to you, and you shall celebrate it as a feast to the Lord; throughout your generations you are to celebrate it as a permanent ordinance. Seven days you shall eat unleavened bread, but on the first day you shall remove leaven from your houses;" *[Exodus 12:13-14]*

The reason they were to eat bread that was not leavened was because leaven was symbolic of untruth and sinfulness. That is why they were to remove, on the first day of the feast, all leaven from their houses. It was meant to teach us the importance of repentance, the need to remove anything that is displeasing to God from our lives.

It certainly did not mean that God wants folks to prove their commitment to Him by eating flat, dry bread for seven days (at least, that is how this guy who grew up on Italian bread might view it). Like so many other things we see in the Bible, it really was not about the bread at all. There was always a spiritual aspect to these teachings, just as there was always a spiritual lesson to be learned from the parables of Jesus, the Master Storyteller. He was "uttering things hidden since the foundation of the world."

In Him, that which was once hidden has now been revealed. Praise God.

The big picture I take away from this little Bible story about yeast, is that many things that God made can be used both for good or for bad, depending on who is using them and for what purposes. Are apples bad? Of course not, especially, not Golden Delicious apples (my favorite). But an apple was certainly used to bring pain and suffering into our world through sin. And the Bible is full of other examples of this, as well. Fire. Rain. Music. Words...just to name a few.

Let's just say, as a good rule of thumb, that it is never what God makes that is bad or sinful. But the potential for good and evil is there in much of what He made. We decide how it is used, usually after some coaxing from the Deceiver (whether we know it or not at the time).

And so it is with leaven, spiritually speaking.

STORY TWENTY-ONE

"Something Hidden, Happily Found"

"The kingdom of heaven is like a treasure hidden in the field, which a man found and hid again; and from joy over it he goes and sells all that he has and buys that field." [Matthew 13:44]

ZOOMING IN

Continuing down the path of talking about things that were hidden, now being revealed or found, our Master Storyteller shines more light on the subject with this parable, but again, from a slightly different angle.

My father was a structural ironworker for many years. In fact, he became the head of the Ironworkers Union in Cleveland, Ohio, for the latter part of his working career. So, growing up, it was gently conveyed to me that maybe following in his footsteps (which I later did for twenty-two years, right out of high school) would not be his first choice for me. Like most fathers, he wanted something better for his son.

So, for awhile, back in high school, I entertained the thought of being an architect. What a tribute that would have been to my Dad, to stay in the same line of work, somewhat, by still being involved in the construction of buildings and bridges, etc., but doing so from the designing side of things, not the actual physical labor part.

I was already intrigued by the construction process, as Dad had often taken us to see the projects he was working on, to show us what they were building. That gave me a taste for seeing something rising up out of the ground, then watching them grow

117

into these amazing structures sometimes ten or twenty stories tall. Some were even taller than that. So, I thought it would really be interesting to be involved in designing something like that and seeing it through to fruition. But, of course, life took me in a different direction.

I did end up taking a drafting course for a couple of years to see if I was cut out to be an architect. And one of the things we studied was something called "orthographic projection." That was where you looked at a three-dimensional object and you would try to draw it in a two-dimensional way. To do this, you would do a number of drawings of the object, but from different views. . . front, back, top, left side and right side. It was the only way to get a full understanding of what the object truly looked like, using only two-dimensional images. I believe Jesus was doing sort of an "orthographic projection" of his word pictures in this cluster of parables, by giving the people a couple of different looks at various aspects of the same subject, "the kingdom of heaven." Try doing that with just a two-dimensional drawing.

The interesting thing about drawing up multiple views of the same object, is that if you are just looking at something from one side, it is almost impossible to envision what the object looks like, as a whole. Take a megaphone, for instance. If you just look at the front of it, squarely on it's face, all you would see is a circle. You would have no way of knowing that the size of that circle gets gradually smaller as you move towards the back end of it. That is why having one or more additional views can be so important. Having a side view, and possibly a rear view, would bring the whole object to light.

Now, we have talked about these small, one verse parables before and they can pack a pretty good punch, for sure. But we also have to be careful, because due to the shortness of the story, it does not give us a lot of detail, which could lead to misinterpretation in some cases, because there are plenty of gaps we need to fill in, by ourselves (hopefully with the help of the Holy Spirit), to try and understand what the Master Storyteller is saying.

This leads me to touch on another strategy Jesus used, in the sharing of these "teaching moments." I believe He sometimes left a little "wiggle room" in His stories to allow each individual listener the opportunity to get a personal revelation from it. He might be trying to show me one thing, and you, something completely different (which leads me to share an interesting story that has developed during the editing process for this book.) It is time for the author to eat a little bit of "humble pie," here. It's okay, though, this is not my first time. . . not by a long shot. If it makes the book better, let's do it.

So, before I sent in the first draft of this book, I had read each chapter multiple times and was fairly confident that my research and my takes on these different parables were pretty solid. But, when I got the notes back from the editor, she pointed to this part of this chapter, the part you are reading right now, and she seems sort of concerned about how I unpacked this little side story.

I have read this parable many times and I always thought that the man, when it says he "sold all that he had and bought the field," sold the treasure he found, too. I thought of the treasure he had found, as now being part of "all that he had,". . . so it would have been part of what he sold. Maybe, he had found a large chunk of gold, and realized there was likely a lot more gold in that field, so he was willing to sell the chunk of gold to get the money to buy the whole field. It seemed to make sense to me, and honestly, the parable really doesn't give us enough information about this treasure. We know he hid what he found, at least at first. But does he eventually sell it? It really doesn't say.

She, in a very gentle and loving way, sort of brought my attention to the fact that my understanding, as I described it, might be wrong. And what do you know? I went back and did a little more research, dug a little deeper and found out that most Bible scholars do not believe that this man sold the treasure he found. He hid it, sold everything else he owned to get the money to buy the field.

Sooooo. . . what you are reading here, now, is my rewrite of this part of the chapter. Thank you to the editor, for having such a keen eye and bringing it to my attention. But the truth is, this happens a lot with the Bible. Five people can read the same passage and get five different meanings. That is definitely the danger of a "one-verse parable." Or is it?

Maybe the Lord intended the story to be just vague enough to allow different people to see it differently, while at the same time, making it precise enough that the moral of the story is the same, for everyone who reads it. Wouldn't that be just like our Master Storyteller, to allow a little room for interpretation, there, to give the Holy Spirit a chance to work. In fact, I think that is quite incredible, actually. How about you?

ZOOMING OUT

Let me take a stab at whipping up a spiritual lesson out of this, one that hopefully is similar to the main point our Master Storyteller was trying to make. I would like to use the writer of this very gospel, Matthew (also known to some as Levi), as the main character for my explanation. Not that Jesus was referring to Matthew, but He could have been. It would seem to fit the story.

Matthew was a tax collector, before meeting Jesus of Nazareth. Tax collectors were known to be greedy, dishonest and usually quite rich in those days. I am not suggesting they were all that way, of course, but that was the perception.

Just look at the story that followed Matthew's conversion. He invites Jesus and the other Disciples over to his home to have dinner. The Pharisees immediately get wind of this and begin accusing Him of hanging out with tax collectors and others of questionable character. Remember when Jesus talked about the physician coming for those who are sick, not those who are well? It was the Pharisees who said, ***"Why is your Teacher eating with the tax collectors and sinners?"*** They were implying that if He was such a holy man and such a great teacher, He should know better than to hang around with this lot.

They did not know that Matthew had just found a hidden treasure, one with great eternal value. And they certainly did not realize that he was going to end up selling all that he had, even walking away from his lucrative business, to follow this man who he believed to be God in the flesh. The Pharisees certainly did not understand all of that. They were just judging him at face value, looking for some reason to accuse Him and discredit Him before the people.

But, Matthew got a taste of the Kingdom, by interacting with our Lord, albeit a small taste at first. But He knew in his heart there was a lot more where that came from and he wanted all of it. So much so, that he was willing to give up all that he had worked for to receive the fullness of it, when his time on Earth was through.

I think that pretty much describes what the Master Storyteller was trying to communicate. Don't you?

STORY TWENTY-TWO

"Diamonds and Pearls"

"Again, the kingdom of heaven is like a merchant seeking fine pearls, and upon finding one pearl of great value, he went and sold all that he had and bought it." [Matthew 13:45-47]

This is now the sixth straight story dealing with some "hidden things" that the Master Storyteller was choosing to reveal, as the psalmist wrote about. It would seem to me, that since all these parables are describing what the Kingdom of Heaven is like, Jesus must be trying to show us that there are many aspects of His Kingdom, most of which had remained hidden until He arrived on the scene. It is like a verbal version of the orthographic projection we discussed.

We still are looking at the same object, the Kingdom, and this is now the sixth view of it, with one more to go after we finish this one. Our Lord has certainly been called a lot of things by a lot of different people. But, let me see if I can add one more to the list. Thorough, He was very thorough. He was not leaving a lot of gaps in His stories for others to fill in or twist. He made Himself extremely clear, and then explained a little more just to make sure He was answering some of their questions before they were even asked.

ZOOMING IN

In the last story, a man found a hidden treasure, took it and hid it where only he could find it again. Then he took all he had, and bought the field where the treasure was found, just in case there was more where the first one came from, I'm guessing.

This story has a slightly different twist to it. A merchant, someone who makes money by buying and selling things of value, comes across this very rare pearl that is worth a lot of money. So much so, that this merchant sells everything he has and buys this pearl. But interesting enough, the Master Storyteller says nothing about him reselling this pearl for a profit.

Those who know me know that I am a huge Beatles fan. My musical endeavors all were inspired, early on, by the Beatles coming to America and playing on the Ed Sullivan show. And I am not the only one. Millions of musicians in my age group, all over the world, would say the same thing. It was a tremendously impactful event that changed not only the music scene forever, but clothes, hairstyles and even the culture we live in, itself. Still, over fifty years later, the radio is still playing their music (in fact, this month...May 2017...Sirius XM Radio is launching a Beatles Channel, a whole channel playing nothing but Beatles music...incredible) and their albums are still being re-mastered, repackaged and are selling like hotcakes. So, you should not be surprised that in 2005, a handwritten copy of the words to "All You Need Is Love" sold at an auction for 1.25 million dollars. It is quite obvious that the collector who bought it, believed that he had found a "pearl of great value." Although, I would wager he plans to make a profit from it at some point, one way or the other. I am not saying there is anything wrong with that, mind you. The Bible encourages wise investing.

People have often been willing to mortgage their houses or sell all that they had for a chance to get even richer. And many times, they lost their life savings doing so. But it does not appear that profit was the motive for this merchant who bought the pearl in our story, because we do not hear of him reselling it. That should be a major tip-off, I would think, that the Master Storyteller is talking about something very unique here, not something you would find every day. But what is also interesting to me, is why Jesus decided to choose a pearl of great value. Why not a diamond? If He found a truly unique and different diamond, that would probably be worth a lot more than the pearl, wouldn't you think?

Let me share this explanation, from Pearls.com, about how a natural pearl is made:

Natural pearls form when an irritant - usually a parasite and not the proverbial grain of sand - works its way into an oyster, mussel, or clam. As a defense mechanism, a fluid is used to coat the irritant. Layer upon layer of this coating, called "nacre" is deposited until a lustrous pearl is formed.

So, let me see if I can come up with a reason as to why a pearl was used, and not a more expensive diamond, for this parable. First of all, I love that it says the whole process is caused by "an irritant," something bad causing something really good. That is so God, right? And we know that diamonds are made from carbon, which after many years of extreme heat and compression, far below the surface of the Earth, becomes this hardened stone worthy of becoming a diamond.

But some very talented people will have to be involved to make that piece of hardened carbon into a priceless diamond. If you just hand someone a piece of that carbon, it would not be worth much to them as it is. It would require a great deal of time and expertise to enhance its value, all the chiseling and cutting, making facets that reflect light just in the right way to make it sparkle. It is all pretty amazing, for sure.

Now, the making of a pearl, as we learned, is a much more natural process. It is far more dependent on the Creator, than on mankind, to make it both beautiful and valuable. Jesus was explaining the Kingdom of Heaven here, not the kingdoms of men, so He went with a more natural occurring treasure, one that humbly points to the handiwork of His Father, not a jeweler.

That's my story and I'm sticking to it.

ZOOMING OUT

If we pull back on this one to see how it fits into these other stories about the Kingdom of Heaven, I want to focus on the part that says, "He went and sold all that he had and bought it." In the previous story, the man sold all that he had and bought the field. In the story of the leaven, it only took a little bit to leaven, or change, the whole lump of dough. We are talking about one thing (or ingredient), that when found or used, can drastically transform something or someone…permanently.

But, before that change could take place, they each had to "go all in." The one using the leaven had to subject the whole lump to the process. The man who bought the field sold all that he had to buy it, which undoubtedly changed the trajectory of his life. And the merchant who buys this pearl made a life-altering decision when he found his treasure, as well.

I am going to go out on a limb here and take a shot at guessing what the Master Storyteller's main point was there by telling these three short little stories. Remember, the parables are the "side stories" not the story. They make the main point easier to grasp.

I believe He was telling them, and indirectly all of us, that if you want to experience the Kingdom of Heaven, both here on Earth and in the life after this one, it is going to cost you everything. The Kingdom of Heaven is not a coat or a jacket that you buy and then wear to keep you warm just when it's cold, then hang it in a closet for the summer. Again, similar to marriage, it is a permanent and constant change. Not something you pick up or set aside on a whim.

The Kingdom of Heaven is also not like a new car that you pay a lot of money for (because by driving it, it makes you look or feel successful for a while) and then you sell it years later for a lot less money than you paid for it. No, the Kingdom of Heaven does not have diminishing returns, and it does not rust or wear out over time or from excessive use.

In fact, back in Matthew 6 again, Jesus told us to store up our treasures in Heaven, not in the things of this world:

"Do not store up for yourselves treasures on earth, where moth and rust destroy, and where thieves break in and steal. But store up for yourselves treasures in heaven, where neither moth nor rust destroys, and where thieves do not break in or steal; for where your treasure is, there your heart will be also". [Matthew 6:19-21]

Here, in the "Sermon from the Boat," the Lord is pointing to this man, and this merchant, in these two stories and saying, "These men were very wise. Once you find something with that kind of value, your earthly possessions pale by comparison. You are not giving everything away, as a foolish man might do. No, you are trading up for something that will never lose its value, not in this world, or even the one to come."

He is saying that the Kingdom that He brings into the world, it is worth everything and only the one who doesn't realize its worth, or thinks that what he has now is worth more, becomes the foolish one, in the end.

This parable also points to another well-loved "pearl of wisdom":

Jesus tells us later, in Matthew 16:26, *"For what will it profit a man if he gains the whole world and loses his soul."*

STORY TWENTY-THREE

"Catch Us If You Can"

"Again, the kingdom of heaven is like a dragnet cast into the sea, and gathering fish of every kind; and when it was filled, they drew it up on the beach; and they sat down and gathered the good fish into containers, but the bad they threw away. So it will be at the end of the age; the angels will come forth and take out the wicked from among the righteous, and will throw them into the furnace of fire; in that place there will be weeping and gnashing of teeth." [Matthew 13:47-50]

ZOOMING IN

I found it very interesting that the very last story Jesus told from the boat on the Sea of Galilee, the one about this dragnet, first of all, was a fishing story and second of all, was a story about the End of the Age. I also am going to try very hard not to jump to the obvious illustration of using the classic TV show, "Dragnet" to help with my explanation here. Rather, I am going to try to stick to "Just the facts, ma'am. Just the facts." Oh well, I tried. Sometimes, I just can't help myself.

Let's think back, for just a few seconds on the Parable of the Wheat and the Tares. Remember how the slaves asked the landowner if he wanted them to start picking out the tares now, rather than waiting until harvest time? The landowner's reply was, "No, wait until the harvest time. If you try to pick them out now, you may damage some of the good crop in the process."

Here in this fishing tale, it seems the Lord is applying similar logic. They cast the nets and bring in whatever is caught by

129

the net, not a real selective process there. Then, once the whole catch is brought in, it would be easier to separate the keepers from the ones to be discarded. So, in hindsight then, did the Parable of the Wheat and Tares possibly have an "End Times" application, as well? I would say, "Absolutely."

Whenever we hear the Son of God talking about a harvest, that should be a hint that He is speaking about the End of the world, as we know it, and the spiritual implications of that moment in time. I would hope it would cause each of us to reflect on how that affects our lives, as individuals. Am I wheat or a tare? Am I a fish to be discarded or a keeper? I cannot think of a single question that a person could ask themselves, that would have a more pivotal impact on their own personal future than where they will be spending eternity? It matters…A LOT…I believe.

If I wanted to put my response into another fish story, to keep it with the theme of this chapter, I would have to equate it to Walter, the whopper of a trout from the movie "On Golden Pond." Young Billy and cranky old Norman finally catch Walter, but throw him back, so others (and maybe Norman himself) could have the thrill of catching him again. But they never really bring that part of the story to conclusion, because he never catches Walter again, or finally enjoys the tasty benefit that Walter offered him, a great meal. No, they leave Walter for another day, which is very much like what many of us do with the eternal question, is it not? We catch it, or think about it from time to time, but we throw it back to be caught again another day.

But what if "another day" never comes? What if Walter dies, or worse yet, what if Norman dies before that next time comes, and he never has the pleasure of catching him again? What if we keep putting off the eternal question until the next time it pops into our head and that next time never comes? Would it be wise to put off such a life-altering question until the next time you think about it or the time after that? Here is what the Apostle Paul had to say about this:

"... for He says, 'At the acceptable time I listened to you; And on the day of salvation I helped you.' Behold, now is "the acceptable time," behold, now is "the day of salvation." [2 Corinthians 6:2]

I believe our place in eternity is one of those questions that must be answered sooner rather than later, especially when our Lord and Savior made the answer so readily accessible. It's not like we have to go digging through a field to find a buried treasure or catch a great big net full of fish, which we must then sort through to find "the keepers."

Eternity is just a prayer away and it is found when we call on the name of Jesus Christ and turn to Him with all of our hearts.

Why waste another minute?

Fish fry...anyone?

When Jesus had finished these parables, He departed from there. [Matthew 13:53]

STORY TWENTY-FOUR

"Bread of Heaven"

Jesus said to them, "I am the bread of life; he who comes to Me will not hunger, and he who believes in Me will never thirst."
[John 6:35]

ZOOMING IN

Before leaving the scene, here in Capernaum, I want to jump back over and touch base with our good friend, John, who was the only one to record this tiny little parable. This parable was one with huge implications for our Master Storyteller, going forward.

Many lists do not even include this story as a parable, because as I mentioned earlier, most lists do not include the parables included in the gospel of John. But, based on the widely accepted definition of what constitutes a parable, being a "side story" or a story that comes along side of the main story or matter at hand, I believe it is. Parables are illustrations that help clarify the central message of the story. And as I said earlier, because of the possible problems that this one little sentence fueled, I think it certainly could be argued that the illustration about Jesus being "the Bread of Life," was a side story to the larger looming fact that He was referring to Himself in divine terms. And apparently, it was an effective illustration, too, as evidenced by the fact that it certainly "set the bees a-buzzin'" only a few verses later.

Therefore, the Jews were grumbling about Him, because He said, "I am the bread that came down out of heaven." They were saying, "Is not this Jesus, the son of Joseph, whose father and mother we know? How does He now say, 'I have come down out of heaven?' " [John 6:41-42]

But, let's go back to the beginning of this chapter, and look at what set the stage for this controversial side story from our Master Storyteller.

Jesus had just returned from Tiberias, on the other side of the sea, where He had fed the five thousand with only two fish and five barley loaves. Needless to say, word was spreading fast. The crowd, wanting to hear more from this Jesus, had jumped into small boats and followed Him back to Capernaum. The Lord responded to the crowd in the following way:

"Truly, truly, I say to you, you seek Me, not because you saw signs, but because you ate of the loaves and were filled. 27 Do not work for the food which perishes, but for the food which endures to eternal life, which the Son of Man will give to you, for on Him the Father, God, has set His seal." [John 6:26-27]

So, as you can see, the issue of food that could lead to eternal life had already been introduced. Then they began to ask Him for a sign, as if somehow feeding five thousand people with only two fish and five loaves of bread was not enough proof. Here is how Jesus responded:

"Our fathers ate the manna in the wilderness; as it is written, 'He gave them bread out of heaven to eat.'" Jesus then said to them, "Truly, truly, I say to you, it is not Moses who has given you the bread out of heaven, but it is My Father who gives you the true bread out of heaven. For the bread of God is that which comes down out of heaven, and gives life to the world." [John 6:31-33]

When the crowd replied, "Lord, always give us this bread," it is fair to say I would think, that they hung a fastball over the middle of the proverbial plate and the Master Storyteller was quite ready to pounce and send into the centerfield seats. He basically said, "You're looking at Him. I am that bread and it is My Father who sent Me."

As if He hadn't already placed Himself in the crosshairs of those who wanted Him gone in the political and religious communities, this was not going to cause them to snuggle up to Him or his heretical message (in their eyes). There is an old saying, "When the hole you're standing in only seems to be getting deeper, stop digging!" Jesus had no intention of stopping. He had a mission to fulfill and that hole was going to get much deeper, plenty deep enough to bury a man, in fact.

ZOOMING OUT

You might be asking yourself why I chose to include this parable from John, one that some would say is not even on the list as a Parable of Jesus, in with the more well-known stories that our Lord shared from that boat, in Matthew, Chapter Thirteen?"

Well, for one, it was up next as we moved forward through the chronology of the Lord's earthly ministry. It came shortly after the ones we just talked about, and shortly before the ones that we will be talking about next, in Luke 10 and beyond.

But more importantly, I felt the Master Storyteller was still unpacking this whole idea of "Kingdom Answers." He had been talking about what it takes to produce a great harvest. Things like good soil, quality seed, keeping the weeds under control and then after the crop is harvested, separating the good yield from the bad.

And all of that, in the cases of wheat and barley (which we have been talking about), leads to the good stuff being ground into flour which, when it is mixed with a little leaven and other ingredients, results in dough that will rise quite nicely, producing fresh and delicious bread. So, what better way to cap off those lessons on good farming practices, with a story about the end result? The bread. Yum.

And the Master Storyteller is not just launching into a story about any ol' bread, here. He is talking about bread that once you eat it, you will never hunger again. Double yum. Then, He reminds us that He had already referred to Himself as the water that quenches your thirst, permanently. So, this one man was claiming to be both the bread and the water that satisfies, once and for all time, for all of eternity, in fact.

No wonder one of my favorite authors of all time, C. S. Lewis, felt compelled to write the following words in his timeless classic, "Mere Christianity":

"I am trying here to prevent anyone saying the really foolish thing that people often say about Him: I'm ready to accept Jesus as a great moral teacher, but I don't accept His claim to be God. That is the one thing we must not say. A man who was merely a man and said the sort of things Jesus said would not be a great moral teacher. He would either be a lunatic — on the level with the man who says he is a poached egg — or else he would be the Devil of Hell. You must make your choice. Either this man was, and is, the Son of God, or else a madman or something worse. You can shut Him up for a fool, you can spit at Him and kill Him as a demon or you can fall at His feet and call him Lord and God, but let us not come with any patronizing nonsense about His being a great human teacher. He has not left that open to us. He did not intend to."

I am not sure I can make it any clearer than that. I am not even going to try. He said it about as plain as it can be said, I think. Jesus Christ was either a liar, a lunatic, or Lord. He was willing to take that risk, when He said such things, because as I said earlier, He was intent on drawing those who were His and repelling those who never would be. He was putting in the winnowing fork, to separate the wheat from the chaff, and to reveal the good fish from among the bad.

But He was also trying to differentiate between the good soil and the bad. The soil that would receive the good seed and bear much fruit and the bad soil that was rocky and hard and left the seed sitting right on top, making it "easy pickin's" for those pesky birds.

But, as C.S. Lewis pointed out, the choice is ours to make. We can't blame God or anyone else. We have been given free will to choose to believe and follow Christ, or reject Him. And Scripture clearly teaches that there is no middle ground.

So, are you good soil? Or are you bad soil? And if you believe you are the latter, are you willing to make a change? A little time and preparation can work wonders, if your heart is willing.

PART FOUR

"Lost and Found"

"I will utter things hidden...
since the creation of the world."

Matthew 13:35

STORY TWENTY-FIVE

"All You Need Is Love"

Jesus replied and said, "A man was going down from Jerusalem to Jericho, and fell among robbers, and they stripped him and beat him, and went away leaving him half dead. And by chance a priest was going down on that road, and when he saw him, he passed by on the other side. Likewise, a Levite also, when he came to the place and saw him, passed by on the other side. But a Samaritan, who was on a journey, came upon him; and when he saw him, he felt compassion, and came to him and bandaged up his wounds, pouring oil and wine on them; and he put him on his own beast, and brought him to an inn and took care of him. On the next day, he took out two denarii and gave them to the innkeeper and said, 'Take care of him; and whatever more you spend, when I return I will repay you.' Which of these three do you think proved to be a neighbor to the man who fell into the robbers' hands?" And he said, "The one who showed mercy toward him." Then Jesus said to him, "Go and do the same." [Luke 1-:30-37]

As we begin our journey into Part Four of this book, it appears we have turned a corner. If Part Three was, to some degree, a halfway point, then we have recalibrated, as my GPS likes to do so often, and we are now making a sweeping turn and heading for home, not only with regards to the reading of this book, but hopefully in our spiritual journey, as well. And thank you, again, for coming along on this adventure. Trust mc, I am learning every bit as much through the writing of this book, as you are by reading it. It is what makes writing so much fun, for me. It forces me dig deeper into God's Word and to do secondary research, as well, which also adds color and meaning to the topics we are covering here. I am just trying to do my best to share the nuggets I find with you. May we all, with God's help, be better because of it.

ZOOMING IN

So, we are turning our attention now to Brother Luke, the good doctor. He is going to handle this part of our tour through the parables. But, before I focus in on the first carrot from this bunch, I would like to jump back to the very first chapter of Luke's gospel to share a few verses that I think say an awful lot about the man and the writings he felt led to share with us:

Inasmuch as many have undertaken to compile an account of the things accomplished among us, just as they were handed down to us by those who from the beginning were eyewitnesses and servants of the word, it seemed fitting for me as well, having investigated everything carefully from the beginning, to write it out for you in consecutive order, most excellent Theophilus; so that you may know the exact truth about the things you have been taught. [Luke 1:1-4]

Two things jumped out at me from Luke's introductory statements here. First, I love his attention to detail. He gives credit to those who compiled this important information before him. But, I guess as a doctor, he felt his experience at doing thorough investigations and asking the right questions might reveal some finer points that could strengthen the case for Jesus being the Messiah, And, secondly, I really liked the fact that he saw a need to write things down as they happened, chronologically, just as I have attempted to do in this book. As much as I love the gospel of Matthew, we did find some curious matters regarding the order of things, did we not? That's why I greatly appreciate Luke's diligence, reporting things in an orderly fashion. I do think it helps to clarify the mission that our Lord was given by revealing the pre-planning and intentionality of His work and ministry. A good storyteller always pays close attention to the order and the flow of events. It just makes the story all that much better.

As we look at this side story in particular, I admit I was tempted to break this one up into two or three chapters, just because there are so many moving parts at work here. We have a man doing some travelling who was beat up, stripped, robbed and left for dead on the side of the road. Then we hear about two "religious leaders," one was a Priest and the other was a Levite (which I confess did remind me of an old joke, but I will spare you the details...as this is a serious subject we are talking about).

Then along comes this Samaritan man...wait...hold on...stop the presses! Didn't we learn, back in story three with the woman at the well, that these Samaritans were a questionable bunch? And now, this man from Samaria is going to stop and help this man who was nearly beaten to death, when two so-called religious men crossed over to the other side of the street and kept walking, as if nothing had happened or at least they pretended not to see it, which is just as bad. What are we to make of this? One might be tempted to say, "Well it just proves that there are some good people everywhere, even in bad neighborhoods, even in a place like Samaria." And I think that would be a good point, one I would agree with.

But, I still think we need to dig a little deeper than that. If we keep reading, he did not just stop and help him by the side of the road. He bound up his wounds, put him onto his own donkey and took him to an inn, where he could rest and recover. He even gave the innkeeper some money to take care of him and said, "If it's more than that, let me know. I'll repay you for your troubles." This guy was not just a good Samaritan, if you ask me, he was a great Samaritan. He went the extra mile and then some, by anyone's estimation, I would say. Wouldn't you?

But we have another first here in this parable. The Master Storyteller actually asks the person He is talking to (a lawyer who was testing Him) a question in response to his question. And it even was a multiple-choice question. I love it. So then, He asks, which of the three proved to be a good neighbor to this man who was suffering? The Priest, the Levite or the Samaritan? I might have even asked the lawyer another question, "What would you have done in that situation?" But, Jesus knows what is in our hearts, so he already knew the answer to that one.

The lawyer responded, "The one who showed mercy toward him." Jesus then responded, *"Go and do the same."* Once again, the Master Storyteller is able to reduce things down to the lowest common denominator and get to the bottom line, boom, just like that.

K.I.S.S. . . keep it simple, Sam!! Show mercy.

ZOOMING OUT

The title of this part of the book is, "Lost and Found." We have moved beyond the initial announcement that "All Things Are New," beyond the "Mounting Questions" and passed all those incredible "Kingdom Answers." We apparently are about to get down to business. And the business that God Almighty is in, is the business of redemption. Here, we are getting our first evidence of this part of the story being revealed by, of all things, a Samaritan man. Is that not just like our Lord? In His eyes, the least among us shall be the greatest. Not the other way around, as we see in the wicked, selfish world we live in.

I have heard it said many times, although I am not sure where the quote originated from, "If God is nothing else, He is always first and foremost, redemptive." His ultimate goal is redemption. Always was and always will be. He is love, for Heaven's sake. And what is love, real love, eternal love, unconditional love, the kind of love that only God is capable of, if it is not totally redemptive, plus or minus nothing.

That is what we are going to be talking about a lot, over these next seven or eight chapters, God's never ending, never changing, always the same, yesterday, today and forever. . . LOVE.

No, that is not just the name of a show about the music of The Beatles in Las Vegas. It is so much more than that. And when we are done talking about it, we will have only scratched the surface because there is no way that any of us, while we are still limited by our earthly minds and bodies, can ever fully comprehend God's love.

STORY TWENTY-SIX

"You've Got a Friend"

Then He said to them, "Suppose one of you has a friend, and goes to him at midnight and says to him, 'Friend, lend me three loaves; for a friend of mine has come to me from a journey, and I have nothing to set before him'; and from inside he answers and says, 'Do not bother me; the door has already been shut and my children and I are in bed; I cannot get up and give you anything.' I tell you, even though he will not get up and give him because he is his friend, yet because of his persistence he will get up and give him as much as he needs. [Luke 11:5-8]

ZOOMING IN

In the first story from this bunch, we looked at a situation where a stranger came to the aid of someone he never met before in his life and he showed great compassion for him, even though others who should have, did not. Now we come to a story with a similar lesson to be learned, this time relating to a friend. That should be much easier, right? Well maybe, but there could be other factors involved like the time of day or night that the friend comes a-knockin'.

You would think that if this person was truly a friend, that the time of day or night would not make much difference. I guess that would be true until someone knocks on your door in the middle of the night and you need to get up early for work in the morning. That might test your otherwise enduring patience. Under your breath you might be saying, "Well, if he was truly a friend, he would not come knocking on my door at that time of night." It's always easier for us to say, "He should have been more kind and understanding," or whatever, until we are the one whose friendship is being tested.

At first glance, this story may not sound like one that fits in with the concept of "Lost and Found." But, if we think about it from the perspective of this person at the door being lost, meaning that he did not even have enough food to offer to one of his friends who came to his house after a long journey, that might qualify. Maybe he had lost his job, or lost his health, but in one way or another it seems he was without good options at the moment. I would consider that lost. The question is, will the person behind the door be a finder, to some degree, in that he would be willing to offer some help? Or would he allow his friend to remain stranded in the middle of a difficult situation, just because he didn't cry out for help at a more convenient time of day?

Let me run another scenario by you and see what you think. You are alone in your car on business trip, heading for Louisville Kentucky, let's say. And about one hundred miles before you reach your destination, you see a man on the side of the road with a sign, "Need a ride to Louisville, can you help?" When I was a lot younger, I might have been inclined to stop and pick him up. Today, I would feel bad about it, but I would keep driving. Not because I wasn't willing to help, but because in this day and age it really is not safe to be picking up hitchhikers. Plus now, in many states, it is illegal to pick up hitchhikers. It is not my generosity that would be in question, but rather my desire to get back home alive. Do you see what I mean? These types of things generally are multifaceted in nature and usually not just a simple choice of being generous or not.

I'd also like to share another verse that might be important to think about, while we are on this subject, from the writer of Hebrews (who many believe to be the same writer, Luke, who recorded this parable, how cool is that?).

Do not neglect to show hospitality to strangers, for by this some have entertained angels without knowing it. [Hebrews 13:2]

Just for the sake of our discussion, I wanted to toss this log onto the fire. What if that person who was needing a ride to Louisville was really an angel sent by the Lord to test you? Now, I am not suggesting you should ever put yourself in a dangerous position or be reckless about your own safety. In fact, let's just remove the personal safety question from the equation for a minute and just look at the possibility that God might sometimes use a stranger (as he did in the last parable) or even someone we know (as in this one) to test us or in some cases, even to protect us from a danger we cannot see.

I would consider such people to be an angel of sorts, or at least someone God was using to minister to us in some way, much like an angel would. Many people have said they were pulled from a wreckage or out of a fiery building by someone they did not know. But once they were safe, that person was gone, never to be seen again. How do you explain that?

My reason for including that example is that I believe it adds to the importance for all of us, especially those who profess faith in Jesus Christ, to be praying regularly and to be walking in the Spirit. If you are connected spiritually, I believe your sensibilities in these kinds of situations will be much more reliable. If you submit your ways to God in your heart on a daily basis, and ask Him to lead you and guide you by the power of the Holy Spirit, I believe that makes it a lot easier to make those judgment calls in the spur of the moment. It is like the old adage, "Luck is a byproduct of great preparation." Better to be ready, than sorry.

I trust that if God is indeed looking out for me and guiding me through my day, I will be much more likely to make the right decision without compromising my safety or well-being. Then, if something bad did happen, I would trust God to help me deal with the outcome.

Pray to the Lord...wait on the Lord...and walk with the Lord.

If you apply these three disciplines regularly, you won't go wrong very often.

ZOOMING OUT

I found it very interesting that the Master Storyteller sandwiched this little brain teaser in between teaching the Disciples how to pray (the Lord's Prayer) and His encouragement to them to "ask, seek and knock." In other words, be persistent. Isn't that what this parable was all about, being persistent? Jesus said that the owner of the house was not motivated to give his friend at the door what he needed because he was a friend, but rather because he was persistent.

I think that is a valuable lesson for all of us. Are you in need of help? Are you hurting or struggling? If the answer is "Yes," are you too ashamed to ask for help? How many people do we see in our daily travels, or even at church on Sunday that when we say, "Hi, how have you been?" they say, "Fine, doing great, thanks for asking," when on the inside their world may be turning upside down? I think we all are guilty of that from time-to-time. We need help, or at least could use some, but we don't tell anybody about it until that molehill becomes a mountain. Then, often it is too late.

I believe the reason that the Master Storyteller wedged this story in between the two lessons on prayer is because persistence pays off. God wants us to be persistent. He is a good, good Father. He already knows what we need before we ask, but He loves to hear His children crying out to Him and looking for His help.

By the way, this tendency by God, to be pleased when we show persistency, is not new at all. It has been that way since the beginning. Remember when Jacob wrestled with God throughout an entire night, seeking a blessing. He was very persistent and the Lord rewarded him. Check it out:

Then he (God) said, "Let me go, for the dawn is breaking." But he (Jacob) said, "I will not let you go unless you bless me." So he said to him, "What is your name?" And he said, "Jacob." He said, "Your name shall no longer be Jacob, but Israel; for you have striven with God and with men and have prevailed." [Genesis 32:26-28]

An entire nation now bears the name of the one who was persistent in an early morning wrestling match with God. That's amazing, is it not? I might have guessed God would have punished him for wrestling with Him. He certainly did not, although Jacob did break his hip during the tussle. But that was a small price to pay, compared to the lasting blessings he received.

Did you ever really listen closely to the words to James Taylor's song, "You've Got a Friend?" It sounds to me like something God could have written, Himself. At least the sentiments match up quite nicely:

> *"Close your eyes and think of me,*
> *And soon I will be there,*
> *To brighten up even your darkest night"*

And….then there's:

> *"Winter, spring summer or fall...all you've got to do is call,*
> *And I'll be there, yeah, yeah, yeah, you've got a friend"*

See what I mean? That could have easily been one of David's psalms, or another of parable from our Master Storyteller.

It fits right in there.

STORY TWENTY-SEVEN

"Where You Lead, I Will Follow"

"Truly, truly, I say to you, he who does not enter by the door into the fold of the sheep, but climbs up some other way, he is a thief and a robber. But he who enters by the door is a shepherd of the sheep. To him the doorkeeper opens, and the sheep hear his voice, and he calls his own sheep by name and leads them out. When he puts forth all his own, he goes ahead of them, and the sheep follow him because they know his voice. A stranger they simply will not follow, but will flee from him, because they do not know the voice of strangers." This figure of speech Jesus spoke to them, but they did not understand what those things were which He had been saying to them.... "I am the good shepherd; the good shepherd lays down His life for the sheep."
[John 10:1-6;11]

ZOOMING IN

I think we will let Brother Luke go on a much-needed lunch break, for a while here, and call on our Brother John again, since this well-known parable is next up in the chronology. Jesus is back in Jerusalem now and has already had a few run-ins with the religious and political leaders who were trying to trip Him up in one way or another.

They really weren't concerned if He was right or wrong, that much. They were more concerned about keeping control over the people for their own selfish purposes. Control equals power and power equals profit. Their religious traditions, although treasured and sincere for the most part, were quite the "cash cow" and they certainly didn't mind being treated like royalty by the common folks, even if the people were more afraid of them than fond of them. The majority would stick with them, right or wrong, rather than buck the traditions of their fathers. Besides, fear is a great motivator and you didn't want to be butting heads with the Jewish leaders, or the Romans, for that matter. If you did, I'm sure there would be a steep price to pay.

If the Jews were nothing else, they were very loyal to their own kind. But this Jesus, He was rocking the boat a little too much for their liking and they were bound and determined to make Him pay for that, which of course they eventually did. His presence, in the meantime, made them very nervous. What if the people sided with Him and began questioning everything the Jewish leaders were teaching them (and some already were)? What then?

This illustration of a shepherd and his sheep was a very fitting one for our Lord to use, at this point in the underlying story. The Jewish people were very much like sheep and easily led, sometimes to a fault. Throughout history, they were led away from God, back towards God and then away again, many times over at the whim of whoever the king was at the time. So, when Jesus called Himself the Good Shepherd and talked about how His sheep would know His voice and follow Him and no one else, you knew the "powers that be" would not be happy and they were not about to take this sitting down. No, they wanted this troublemaker silenced and the sooner the better.

Think of the irony here. Jesus is saying, "My sheep know My voice and they follow Me." And then John writes that, "This figure of speech Jesus spoke to them, but they did not understand. . . ." What does that say about these religious leaders, then? If they were not "His sheep" and they were not willing to follow His voice, then the people were going to have to make a choice. They never really had to worry about that before. Oh, this was not good, not good at all. . . but wait, there was more.

There was yet another sandal to drop. Jesus finishes with the statement that, "The good shepherd lays his life down for the sheep." Of course, He knew what was going to happen, in the not too distant future, but the Pharisees did not. They were not the type of leaders to jump to the front and be willing to die for the cause. But now, if they killed Jesus, they would only be making His argument stronger. Oh, this Master Storyteller was good, really good. He was beating them at their own game and they did not like it one bit.

You see, the Jewish people knew all about shepherds. Joseph, with his coat of many colors, was a shepherd. Jacob was a shepherd. David was a shepherd. And they knew the prophecies suggesting that they, like sheep, had gone astray and that one day God would send the True Shepherd, the One who would lead them to those green pastures that David wrote about, once and for all. They also knew all the prophecies about how the promised Messiah was to come. He would be born in Bethlehem, as David was. He would be a descendant of David, Son of Jesse. He would also come with power and authority, and the people had already seen many examples of that.

The puzzle was starting to take shape and more and more people were starting to realize that this Jesus might in fact be the Promised One. After all, the name Jesus which was translated from the Hebrew name Joshua, and means "Jehovah is salvation" and Mary was instructed to name Him Jesus. It, at least, was getting harder and harder to just dismiss Him as a heretic or just a troublemaker.

Plus, it was only a short time before He would say this to the Jews, "Before Abraham was, I AM." And once He had said that, they picked up stones, and intended to kill Him for heresy. The name, "I AM" was not thrown around lightly among the Jews, because when Moses asked God what His name was, He answered, *"I am who I am"* and *"I AM has sent me (Moses) to you."* Red flags were being raised all over the place once Jesus said that. They immediately thought, "This man just claimed to be God."

So, to now say, I am the Good Shepherd and the sheep know My voice and follow Me," He really was signing His death certificate, and He knew that too. But, He was the Lamb of God, the One who would take away the sins of the world. He had a mission to fulfill and nothing either in Heaven or on Earth was going to stop Him from completing the task

After all, Jesus Christ was the incarnate Word of God and God's Word never fails to accomplish His purposes.

ZOOMING OUT

"The Lord is my shepherd, I shall not want. He makes me lie down in green pastures; He leads me beside quiet waters. He restores my soul; He guides me in the paths of righteousness for His name's sake. Even though I walk through the valley of the shadow of death, I fear no evil for You are with me." [Psalm 23:1-4]

I didn't think it would be right to finish this chapter on the Good Shepherd without talking about maybe the most famous reference to a shepherd in the entire Bible. You have probably attended plenty of funerals where they read the Twenty Third Psalm as a way of helping those who are grieving over the loss of a loved one to believe that he or she is in a better place. It is a beautiful picture to ponder, for sure. The peace, the quietness, the restoring of one's souls and maybe the best part of it all, the absence of fear and suffering.

If there is a better illustration of true redemption, I can't think of one. Sheep who were given up for lost, because they had wandered away from the fold, whether it was by their own choice that they had wandered or they were led astray by a bad shepherd, they would all be considered lost. But David paints this picture of peace, tranquility and redemption where the Lord, our ultimate Shepherd, leads His sheep by the green pastures and the still waters of His eternal Kingdom. The ultimate hope is that all the lost sheep will one day be found again, forgiven, and brought back into the Father's fold, never to stray again. May it be so, Lord. Amen.

I would like to end this chapter with another little parable, this one from Matthew 18, where the Good Shepherd reveals more of His ever-loving nature.

"What do you think? If any man has a hundred sheep, and one of them has gone astray, does he not leave the ninety-nine on the mountains and go and search for the one that is straying? If it turns out that he finds it, truly I say to you, he rejoices over it more than over the ninety-nine which have not

gone astray. So it is not the will of your Father who is in heaven that one of these little ones perish." [Matthew 18:12-14]

"So, it is not the will of your Father who is in heaven that one of these little ones perish." Ahhhh. . . that is so awesome. I wanted to repeat that part, so it would sink in. Let's just ponder that thought for a while. He does not want a single one of His sheep to remain lost. What a loving, gracious and redemptive God we serve.

Thank you, Lord.

STORY TWENTY-EIGHT

"Storing Your Treasures Wisely"

And He told them a parable, saying, "The land of a rich man was very productive. And he began reasoning to himself, saying, 'What shall I do, since I have no place to store my crops?' Then he said, 'This is what I will do: I will tear down my barns and build larger ones, and there I will store all my grain and my goods. And I will say to my soul, "Soul, you have many goods laid up for many years to come; take your ease, eat, drink and be merry."' But God said to him, 'You fool! This very night, your soul is required of you; and now who will own what you have prepared?' So is the man who stores up treasure for himself, and is not rich toward God." [Luke 12:16-21]

ZOOMING IN

This could possibly be the shortest chapter in the entire book. The moral of this story is, "You can't take it with you!!" Alrighty then, on to the next chapter.

Aha, gotcha there!! Not so fast, friends. Upon further investigation, there are a number of really interesting things happening in this parable beyond the most obvious one. Let's just start with this one sentence, *"And I will say to my soul, 'Soul, you have laid up for many years to come; take your ease, eat, drink and be merry.' "* When was the last time you had a conversation with your soul and told it to relax, take it easy. . . eat, drink and be merry? Does a soul even eat or drink? I know it can be merry, but I did not think it required food or strong drink to be that way. Is Jesus being a little funny, here? I think so. I think the Master Storyteller, using a little sarcastic humor, was nudging His listeners to dig a little deeper, and maybe ask themselves why this man is talking to His soul in the first place. I think I have come up with two possible scenarios.

First of all, people who are successful and wealthy often like to give themselves most of the credit. If they share it with other people, they might come asking for a raise and that could get costly. Or they could use their success to help them find a better paying job down the street, possibly even with a competitor. Either way, if you are that business owner, you probably won't be fond of either of those options. So why not just give yourself all the credit? You are already being paid very well and you are not leaving to go work for someone else. It makes me think of the old Quaker Oats commercial where the Quaker says, "Nothing is better for thee, than me." I am thinking this rich landowner would more likely look into a mirror and say, "Nothing is better for me...than me!!"

And the second option would be that, well, he is a very wealthy and successful landowner, so how many real friends do you think he might have, at least ones he could trust? It is likely he has alienated a lot of people on his way to the top and the people that are most loyal to him probably are only doing so because he is the boss and they need that job. So maybe, like a lot of rich people do, he walled himself off to protect himself from the leeches. When you have lots of money, they do tend to show up with a hard luck story and a hand out. Good chance this rich man found that out the hard way, so he closed the ranks down to just himself. Sounds pretty sad, right? But it does happen.

The other aspect of this story that I want to touch on is the end part, where God says to him, "You fool! This very night, your soul is required of you."

As I am writing the first draft of this chapter, just two days ago, I found out that a co-worker of mine, a man I knew pretty well, was out celebrating his birthday with friends and somehow before the night was over, sadly he came up missing. He was only 57 years old. He was healthy, happy and things were going great, as far as anyone knew. But in a blink of an eye, it's possible that he left this world much too soon. I certainly hope that is not the case. He was a good man, loved my many.

Another very good friend of mine, was lying in bed with his wife one morning last week (at the time of this writing), they had just awakened and were about to get up and get ready for work. He stretched his arms above his head, made a slight grunting noise, and he became unconscious and died a few day later of what was believed to be a massive heart attack. He and I were the same age, sixty-three. What a shocker. He was much too young, for sure.

But these things happen all the time. I am certain most of you have experienced this with people you have known. Life is fragile and we know that "no man is promised tomorrow." Which is why, as we talked about a few chapters ago, "Today is the acceptable day of salvation." Eternity is something you do not want to procrastinate with. As far as I know, there are no "do-overs" and eternity is a very, very long time.

It would seem to me to be very foolish, to ignore the inevitable, as if it will never come. Especially when we are told over and over that Jesus Christ came to this planet specifically to provide each and every one of us with the redemption and forgiveness necessary to allow us entrance into His kingdom, when this life is through. We are told it will be a Kingdom far beyond anything we can imagine or hope for.

Why would you want to pass on that? It is not like you are being told, "Look, you can live forever, but it will be in Siberia. Honestly, you haven't been all that good. You surely didn't expect the royal treatment, right?" No, not even close, we have an amazingly gracious God who only wants to give the best to His children...all His children.

The only way you will not receive His promises is to reject His invitation. But why would anyone do that? My guess is, only if they are somehow blinded from seeing the big picture. Surely, if they saw and understood what was being offered, no one would refuse. In fact, the Apostle Paul talked about this very problem in his first letter to the Corinthians. Let's talk about that.

ZOOMING OUT

"Things which eye has not seen and ear has not heard and which have not entered the heart of man, all that God has prepared for those who love Him." [1 Corinthians 2:9]

Listen, my friends. Heaven is going to be incredible. No pain, no suffering, no guilt, no temptation and no nighttime. . . only the light of the Lord and the glory of God's presence. It will be like seeing the Garden of Eden restored right before your very eyes, only a thousand times better. What is there to think about? Accept the invitation. Make sure your spot is reserved for the Marriage Feast of the Lamb. You think the wedding of Prince Charles and Princess Diana was "out of this world?" Trust me. It will be like running away and going to the Justice of the Peace, compared to this one. And you are invited. It is not something you will want to miss.

But it is not just all about the "hereafter." I have been a Christian for thirty-eight years, at the time of this writing and I can tell you, being a Christian does not just promise to make the next life better. Having Christ in my life, here on Earth, has made this life a lot better. I don't have the time or space, here, to list all the amazing things that have happened to me since I gave my life to Jesus. But there have been a whole lot of them, and I am still amazed when I look back and realize just how blessed I have been.

Many people have asked me, when we talk about God, religion or the Bible, "How can you base your life on writings in a book that are between two thousand and six thousand years old?" I tell them, "I don't base my life on a book, or a church (although I regularly attend a great one), or anyone who has ever lived before me. And to some degree, it is not even based on the earthly ministry of Jesus Christ, although that was hugely impactful, no doubt.

I base my life on the experiences I have had over the last thirty-eight years, being in a living, breathing, spur of the moment relationship with the Creator of all things. I know Him intimately, and He knows me intimately. I share my darkest secrets with Him (of course, He already knows them). I have placed my life and even my marriage into His hands. I can honestly say that without His involvement in my wife's life and mine, I doubt we would have lasted this long (soon to be forty years, we both came to Christ not long after we were married, talk about a miracle).

And there are so many more miracles I could share, if time and space allowed, not the least of which is our four beautiful children and seven grandkids so far (we recently found out the eighth grandchild is on the way!!). To say I am blessed, that would be a huge understatement. I am constantly humbled and always thankful for God's goodness. It has always exceeded my expectations, by a long shot."

This section of the book is about redemption and things that were lost being found. I was lost and I was found by Christ. My wife, Lauri, was lost and she was found. Millions of people, all around the world today, were once lost and headed down the path that leads to death and destruction and eternal separation from God. But at the right time, like a piece of fruit that is picked at just the perfect amount of ripeness, they were found and redeemed by our Lord and Savior, Jesus Christ. Well, okay, He didn't need to find us. He knew where we were all time, physically and spiritually, but you catch my drift.

The Master Storyteller is more than a just a good "spinner of tales." He is the God who created us, and knows us better than we know ourselves. And He wants more than anything to have a relationship with you that lasts for all of eternity. And He would really like to start right now, if you have not done so already. Why wait?

In the Lord's Prayer, He said we are to pray these words, "Thy Kingdom come, thy will be done on Earth as it is in Heaven." We can start enjoying His kingdom, just as He explained to Nicodemus, right here and right now through His Holy Spirit, which He gives in full when we call on His name and ask Him to be our Lord and Savior. There is really no reason to wait. Sadly, the rich landowner in the story Jesus told did not take the time to do that. At least, that was not part of the story.

The reality is, not all stories or all lives have happy endings. Only the ones that ultimately find their end in the presence of our risen Lord do. And honestly, I love my life, my wife, my kids and all my friends, but I can't wait to be there in that glorious place He is preparing for us. My only prayer is that you all will be there with us.

Now, that is going to truly be a "neverending story" with the happiest of endings. Which is, of course, no ending at all.

STORY TWENTY-NINE

"Figless"

And He began telling this parable: "A man had a fig tree which had been planted in his vineyard; and he came looking for fruit on it and did not find any. And he said to the vineyard-keeper, 'Behold, for three years I have come looking for fruit on this fig tree, without finding any. Cut it down! Why does it even use up the ground?' And he answered and said to him, 'Let it alone, sir, for this year too, until I dig around it and put in fertilizer; and if it bears fruit next year, fine; but if not, cut it down.'" [Luke 13:6-9]

ZOOMING IN

When I read this parable, there is one word that comes to mind. It was used in the Bible, but not one that we use all that often these days, longsuffering. I think it nicely sums up the primary focus of this story. God is longsuffering towards His children, in other words, patient.

And at the start of my observations, here, I want to say in advance that I may be taking some minor liberties with my view of this interesting tale. The things that I share may be a little bit "outside of the box" when compared to the way that most Biblical experts might portray what was happening in the story Jesus told. But I do so, hopefully, to provide some food for thought, even though it seems the tree in this story was not providing much of anything. And therein lies the problem.

I am going to suppose (bear with me) that the conversation that takes place in this interesting parable could be a picture of God the Father talking with Jesus, His Son. Let's think of it, for a moment, as the Father saying, "Behold, for three years I have come looking for fruit on this tree (Israel), without finding any. Cut it down!"

But, before going any further, I want to share another portion of Scripture that may help me explain where I am going with all of this.

"But do not let this one fact escape your notice, beloved, that with the Lord one day is like a thousand years, and a thousand years like one day. The Lord is not slow about His promise, as some count slowness, but is patient toward you, not wishing for any to perish but for all to come to repentance." [2 Peter 3:8-9]

What do you know? A couple of verses penned by Peter about the "longsuffering" nature of the Lord. I think he knew a little bit about that, since Jesus was longsuffering towards him, even though he denied Him three times, right? And what about the "walking on water" thing? Yes, Peter and Jesus had a history, you could say.

But, I also want to focus on this Biblical "rule of thumb" that he is introducing here. For centuries, Biblical scholars have pointed to this verse as a way of interpreting the Bible, especially with regards to timelines, like when the Earth was created and trying to understand the prophetic things concerning the End of the Age.

Is our Master Storyteller pointing to this time measurement tool, here in this story, to help us to see the bigger picture? I believe that might be a reasonable assumption. But bear with me for just another moment, as I share one more verse, this time from Jesus, Himself, that is also a key to understanding what I am talking about. This will all make sense in a minute, I promise.

"But of that day and hour no one knows, not even the angels of heaven, nor the Son, but the Father alone. For the

coming of the Son of Man will be just like the days of Noah.
[Matthew 24:36-37]

Noah? Aren't we a little off the subject. He was born like five thousand years ago. How does that have anything to do with the unfruitful tree in our story. Well, this is where the fun begins.

If we could presume that this parable is symbolic of a conversation between the Father and the Son regarding a fig tree and that tree, of course, has long been symbolic of gods chosen nation, Israel. Isn't it interesting, then, that Jesus describes the man who owned the fig tree as coming and looking for fruit, without finding any for three years? Couldn't we draw a connection, considering the words written by Peter and Matthew, between the three years Jesus spoke of and the three thousand years or so that had elapsed from the days of Noah until the times of Christ?

Let's quickly look at the usual Biblical time line. Most think from Genesis to Christ was approximately four thousand years and we know that from the time of Christ until now is roughly two thousand years. That is a total of six thousand (or six days) and the Bible teaches that when Christ returns, there will be a thousand-year reign, here on Earth, where Satan is bound and the world is free from sin and temptation. That would be the seventh day, or the day of rest. Interesting, is it not? And Noah was born around one thousand years after Adam and Eve, so about three thousand years before Christ. See...now the plot thickens.

Is it possible that Jesus was implying that for three thousand years, since God destroyed the world by a great flood to rid the world of evil, that the new world and the nation that He gave birth to through the seed of Abraham, had not brought forth any fruit and was only worthy of being cut down and destroyed?

Is it also possible that the story points to the Son, who in the New Testament is described as the one Mediator between God and man, asking for a little more time to dig around that tree and put in some fertilizer (may I suggest that could be the Gospel and the Holy Spirit?), to see if He can change the outcome, sparing this tree that the Father loves, the whole tree, from being tossed into the fire as worthless.

Could that really be what the Master Storyteller was alluding to here? Was He saying, it has been three thousand years

167

since the flood and what do you have to show for yourself, nation of Israel, other than numerous rebellions, chasing after other Gods and countless wars and judgments? Was the Lord saying that He had come to give them another chance, that the Father had sent Him to offer a new and different plan of redemption? But it was not an unconditional promise of salvation. There would have to be some fruit (produced by the Holy Spirit), or the end might still be the same. Redemption does not come without a true change in direction, or repentance, if you will.

But where there is true repentance, real redemption is not only possible, it's promised to all. Once again, the choice is yours and mine to make.

ZOOMING OUT

So, this little story about a fig tree that would not produce good fruit, and was facing destruction, seems to be a lesson on individual fruitfulness, when taken at face value. But, when we dig a bit deeper, it turns out that it may have been much more than that. Our God is big on dual meanings. So often, these stories have both immediate relevance and long-term implications, as well, nothing new there.

This one may have been also pointing to a nation, greatly blessed and chosen of God, who had squandered those many blessings, not to mention repeated rebellion and had sought after its own ways. And here, some three thousand years after the Lord hit the restart button on humanity and all that He had created, He came to Earth, Himself, and was prepared to intervene again. But this time, He was making sure that it was understood that it would require a change of direction and really, a change of heart in each and every one of us, if we were to be spared. It was certainly not a blank check, or "carte blanche," as the French say.

Yes, action is required. A decision needs to be made by each of us. Would we be willing to receive what the Son was offering, that we all may finally bear fruit that leads to redemption? Only God knows that answer for sure. But it is a question we all need to answer at some point.

It is also interesting to note how this story ends. The keeper of the vineyard, who I suggest may be the Son in this story, implies that He is going to come again later to see if there has been any fruit. And if not, the tree will be cut down and destroyed.

So, I may be jumping to conclusions here, but it sounds to me like there is coming a day when this keeper is going to return again, looking for fruit that was produced with the help of the Holy Spirit. And if He finds that fruit, He can say, "See Father, this fig tree has produced good fruit and is worthy of escaping the fire."

The good news for you and I is that, as the Apostle Paul wrote, if we believe in Jesus Christ and have been grafted into that fig tree we've come to know as Israel, we have been offered the same eternal fate as the Jew who eventually receives Jesus Christ, by faith, as Messiah and Savior. Here is how he explained it:

But by their transgression salvation has come to the Gentiles, to make them jealous... But if some of the branches (Jews) were broken off, and you, being a wild olive (Gentiles), were grafted in among them and became partaker with them of the rich root of the olive tree (Israel)...You will say then, "Branches were broken off so that I might be grafted in." Quite right, they were broken off for their unbelief, but you stand by your faith. [Romans 11:11, 17, 19-20]

So once again, a story that seemed to be speaking just about fruitfulness and a tree that seemed to have gone bad, is really a story of redemption, both for that original tree, and the new shoot that had been grafted in.

Thanks to the longsuffering of both the keeper of the vineyard and the owner of the trees, patience will likely pay off when that keeper returns again to look for the fruit of His labor.

Thanks be to God.

STORY THIRTY

"Just One Out of A Hundred"

"What man among you, if he has a hundred sheep and has lost one of them, does not leave the ninety-nine in the open pasture and go after the one which is lost until he finds it? When he has found it, he lays it on his shoulders, rejoicing. And when he comes home, he calls together his friends and his neighbors, saying to them, 'Rejoice with me, for I have found my sheep which was lost!' I tell you that in the same way, there will be more joy in heaven over one sinner who repents than over ninety-nine righteous persons who need no repentance. [Luke 15:4-7]

ZOOMING IN

As we begin to look at this classic parable, we see two of the skills that Jesus has used before, as Master Storyteller, now being used together.

First, He is speaking in very clear and understandable terms, using an illustration that the listeners could easily relate to. He's talking about what it means to be a shepherd and what would happen if one of the sheep were to be separated from the rest. By comparison, a lazy shepherd might say, "It is only one sheep. There are ninety-nine more still in the fold. Why should I risk my life and go out into the fields looking for this stray? Something bad could happen to me out there. Also, while I am gone, even more of the sheep might wander off. No, it is better that I stay here and attend to the ones that are still accounted for. That is what I think the master would have me do."

So yes, we see Jesus speaking in common terms, here, as He often did when He was speaking to those who were not "with Him." In this instance, He was speaking to the Pharisees who were questioning Him about hanging out with tax collectors and sinners. So, He wanted to speak plainly, which or course, He did. He knew very well how they loved to misquote or trap Him.

Secondly, many times He would follow up a parable with an explanation or interpretation. Again, He tended to do this more when He was speaking to those who did not "have ears to hear," and that was the case with this story. In fact, as I alluded to earlier, He went even a step farther with this one. He not only spoke in very clear and relatable terms, with the story being about tending to the sheep, in particular a lost one, but He also made sure to give an explanation in the very last sentence, of how this side story pointed to the main issue at hand. Let's look at it again:

"I tell you that in the same way, there will be more joy in heaven over one sinner who repents than over ninety-nine righteous persons who need no repentance." [Luke 15:7]

Wait a minute, who was the Lord talking to here, again? The Pharisees, religious leaders, supposedly the ones who obeyed the letter of The Law most enthusiastically. And now, He is saying that this parable was not about sheep at all, but sinners who strayed and the righteous ones who did not. I can almost hear the defense shields snapping into place as the Lord is talking. They are thinking, "Who is He calling sinners? Is He talking about us, the ones who are doing our best to protect the flock? How dare He question us? If it weren't for us, all the sheep would be lost. If He is who He says He is, He should be thanking us, not talking down to us."

Isn't it funny how sometimes without a word, even if no one is accusing us of anything, we begin to get defensive? I have done it and I suspect most of you have, as well. Some would say that is our own conscience convicting us and making us feel guilty. I like to think of it as the Holy Spirit at work in our hearts. One of the functions of the Holy Spirit is to convict us of our sin. Deep inside, we know we are guilty of committing many sins, but we are very good at suppressing those guilty impulses, sometimes by using our own internal defenses mechanisms. One of those we use most often is pride.

It all started in the Garden, with the serpent and Adam and Eve. The evil one sows a little pride (or leaven) into their hearts by saying, "He just doesn't want you to be like Him. He knows if you eat of this fruit, you will have full knowledge of good and evil and will be able to figure things out for yourself. You won't really need His help, then. That is why He doesn't want you to eat of this tree." Then, they buy into the lie by thinking, "Why shouldn't we be like Him? We should be able to figure things out for ourselves. We don't need God or anyone else to tell us right from wrong. We are able to decide for ourselves." But they knew enough to hide, when God came looking for them, right?

And so it began, and not much had changed over the years. We see the Pharisees doing the same exact thing all over again saying, "Who is He? We don't need Him to preach to us about how to protect our flock. Surely, we know the right thing to do in that situation. We have been doing this our whole lives. Can you believe the nerve of this guy?"

Pride. The very thing they say comes before a fall, just as it did in the Garden of Eden, was still alive and well thousands of years later when Jesus walked among us, and is very much still alive today!

ZOOMING OUT

As we draw closer to the end of this group of stories, it seems that the Master Storyteller is now "zooming in" on the whole subject of sin, rebellion and how we are to turn away from it all, if we are to find redemption and spend eternity with Him. Of course, the subject was not a new one. Isaiah was led of the Lord to speak a very similar message, many years before Christ was born and became the Good Shepherd. Let's take a look at what Isaiah wrote:

All of us like sheep have gone astray,
Each of us has turned to his own way;
But the Lord has caused the iniquity of us all
To fall on Him. [Isaiah 53:6]

173

It seems that God was speaking to "all of us" through the prophet, Isaiah. That would include the tax collectors, the sinners (all kinds) and yes, even the Pharisees. The Lord is what some might refer to as an "equal opportunity offender." He doesn't like to leave anyone out. When He points out our flaws, there is plenty of guilt to go around. We all know what it says in Romans 3, *"For all have sinned and fall short of the glory of God."* At least, most of us have grown up with an understanding that no one is perfect. But the religious leaders of the day, when Christ walked the Earth (and I do not think it is that different today) seemed to hold on to this "security blanket" that they were just a tad bit better than everyone else, because of all the good work they were doing for the Lord.

Interestingly enough, as I was writing this chapter, on television there were images coming from Rome as President Trump had a face-to-face meeting with Pope Francis, the high priest of the Roman Catholic Church. And he had just come from Israel, where he had met with the leaders of the Jewish faith and from Saudi Arabia where he had met with the leaders of fifty Muslim nations. It was historic trip, to say the least. The man referred to (by virtue of his office) as "the leader of the free world," meeting with the leaders of the three most prominent religions of the world, one right after the other. That had never happened before. And it is happening sixty-nine years after Israel becomes a nation, again? Call me crazy, but I am led to believe these things are not trivial or insignificant, if as Jesus said, we are the last generation?

I only mention this, here, because again, very little has changed, even now, during what some would think of as the enlightened times of the modern era. Many would say we have come to a place where we can decide what is right and wrong for ourselves and we don't need God or any religious institution telling us what to think. Yet, the pictures we have seen over the last few days remind us that the majority of people in the world, here in the twenty-first century, still look to highly esteemed religious leaders for direction, for guidance and even to find some sort of peace and redemption.

We see that whether it is an Imam, a Rabbi or the Pope, millions of people look to them for inspiration and hope. And so it was with these Pharisees. They were "puffed up," as with that leaven we talked about, by their own status and success.

But, what Jesus was saying, here, is that God looks at the individual, one at a time. He is suggesting that the one sheep is as important as the ninety-nine, maybe even moreso, because it is lost. That is a huge departure from the major religions of the world that seem to be more fixated on having great numbers of followers. There is nothing wrong with having a great many followers, mind you, just that, it should never be the primary goal of a church. Pointing people to God, that should always be the goal, whether it is ten people or ten million.

We all know what it says in John 3:16, and we talked about that earlier in this book. God sent His Son, that *"whoever believes in Him. . ."* shall not perish but have eternal life. He did not say "any Jew," "any Muslim," or "any Christian." He did not say, "Unless you are an atheist." He said, "whoever."

But when was the last time you took a good look at the very next verse:

For God did not send the Son into the world to judge the world, but that the world might be saved through Him. [John 3:17]

He did not come to judge or punish. The Father sent His Son to become the only true source of redemption and forgiveness, the Lamb that would be sacrificed as payment for sin, once and for all, for all of mankind. Not a building, or a hierarchy or some esteemed person. None of those could provide redemption, only the Son was given that authority. All the others can do is point to Him. Only His work on the Cross was complete, payment in full, with no further sacrifice needing to be offered. Not one lost sheep would be excluded or ignored. He came to seek us all.

Oh, one last point before we move on. Singer, songwriter and evangelist, Keith Green, once had an album called "Songs for the Shepherd." On the cover, Keith is pictured with a little lamb draped over his shoulders. I have always loved that picture. But what does Jesus say in this parable:

175

"When he has found it, he lays it on his shoulders, rejoicing." [Luke 15:5]

What a great thought to end this chapter on. He carries us. Once we come into a relationship with the Good Shepherd, He literally picks us up off the ground, drapes us over His shoulders and carries us home.

Let's just leave it right there and ponder that for a while.

STORY THIRTY-ONE

"Heaven Rejoices Again"

"Or what woman, if she has ten silver coins and loses one coin, does not light a lamp and sweep the house and search carefully until she finds it? When she has found it, she calls together her friends and neighbors, saying, 'Rejoice with me, for I have found the coin which I had lost!' In the same way, I tell you, there is joy in the presence of the angels of God over one sinner who repents." [Luke 15:8-10]

ZOOMING IN

For about forty years, before I decided to try my hand at writing books, my main creative outlet was songwriting and I still do dabble with that even now. I am pretty amazed at the similarities between the two types of writing. Aside from the fact that a song is basically a three-minute composition, short and to the point, and a book is much longer, usually a hundred pages or more and takes a while to read, the approach to both is much the same.

A long time ago, I attended a songwriting seminar where the teacher gave us two tips that have stuck with me for all these years. It's been amazing to see how helpful these two songwriting techniques have been equally useful, as well, to the writing of a book. Here they are:

1)   Always write a song backwards, starting with the main point or destination in mind, and work back from there. Much like planning a vacation, you need to know where you want

to end up, before heading out. If you don't, you could end up somewhere completely different.

2)   Once you come up with the title or hook line, repeat it often. The more people hear it, the more likely they are to remember it.

And wouldn't you know it, the Master Storyteller uses these two strategies in much of His storytelling. (No surprise there). We have talked before about how the Lord liked to bunch up His stories, often with a similar theme or focal point, and repeatedly drive home the moral or lesson He was trying to convey. And I think it is safe to say that He knew very well where He wanted to end up, so He didn't accidentally wander off topic (as I have a habit of doing).

Let's take a look at the hook line or main point Jesus was making in this parable:

"In the same way, I tell you, there is joy in the presence of the angels of God over one sinner who repents." [Luke 15:10]

Hey, wasn't that pretty much the same message in the last sentence of the previous parable, the one about the lost sheep? You got it. Repetition works. Every songwriter, author and teacher knows that. Remember doing those flashcards to help learn your multiplication tables when you were in grade school? Of course, you do. UGGHH.

Moving on, then, the main point of this story is how the angels in Heaven rejoice over one sinner who repents. The side story, or parable, that He uses to illustrate this was first a lost sheep and now, a lost coin. We can all relate to someone losing something of value like a silver coin or gold, right, since not many of us have sheep today. What if your dog ran away? Would you not drop whatever else you're doing at that moment and focus all your attention on finding you precious pup? Of course, you would. I would be more surprised by anyone who would not.

Does God love me as much as I love my dog or some valuable possession? Ummm...I don't know...I really love my dog so...WAIT! What am I saying? Of course, God loves me, and all His children, in fact, every bit as much as I love my dog, actually, far more. That is not to say that I don't love my dog that much. It is just that we, as humans, are incapable of loving anyone or anything as deeply and purely as God loves each of us. He is love, through and through. It is not something He does. It is who He is, period.

So, while Jesus is, once again, boiling this concept down into something we can all relate to, like lost animals or coins, doesn't it make you wonder why He had to break it down for us? Are we that blind to spiritual things, that we would not be able to comprehend it if He just said, "Look, I am love, pure love. So, don't worry, if you wander away from the flock, I am going to drop everything and come after you, and all my angels will be out looking for you until we find you and I drape you over my shoulders and carry you home. And once we do, and we will, I promise. We are going to throw one heck of a party!!"

Okay, I'll speak for myself on this one. I might be like, "Yeah, that sounds really great. But I have had bad luck, before, with things that sound too good to be true. They usually are. So, would you mind giving me an example of something relatable, like a lost sheep or a lost coin? I can wrap my head around that. But, I have a slight problem with the idea of all of Heaven forming a search party, just for me, if I should wander away at some point. Sorry Lord. It's not You, it's me. I am just not sure I am worth all of that trouble."

Sound familiar? No wonder God is abundant in patience and longsuffering. We really are a faithless bunch at times, are we not?

ZOOMING OUT

When we were talking about a lost sheep, we were talking about something that, all on its own, just got up and wandered away. But now, when we read the story about the lost coin, we see an example of something that did not wander away on its own. The owner just misplaced it. If I view this as how it might fit into the overall picture of redemption, I believe I have stumbled onto something, that as Christians, we don't talk about too often. It is something that is commonly referred to as "original sin." Let me explain.

As we have discussed a number of times before, we are all sinners. No one, apart from Jesus Christ, has managed to live on this planet, completing their time here without committing one, or more than likely, many sins. None of us are, based on our own lives and choices, without sin. We are, as they say, "Guilty as charged."

But, what if you were this "freak of nature," who managed to wander through this life for seventy or eighty years or so, without slipping up one single time. No lies, no curse words, no envy, no judging of others (about 99% of us are off the island already, right?) and never once having even an immoral thought. And to top it off, you always treated others better than you treated yourself.

Well listen, if you checked all the boxes, I would really love to meet you. That would be quite an accomplishment (providing your only sin was not being able to be honest with yourself, just kidding). You and Jesus would be all alone at the top of that mountain. I would be down at the bottom with all the other ones who "fell short of His glory."

Would that mean, then, that you were able to enter Heaven based on your own diligence and hard work, in other words, you earned it? (Not exactly). Let's see what the Apostle Paul had to say about this subject:

> *Therefore, just as through one man sin entered into the world, and death through sin, and so death spread to all men, because all sinned...for until the Law sin was in the world, but sin is not imputed when there is no law. Nevertheless, death reigned from Adam until Moses, even over those who had not sinned in the likeness of the offense of Adam, who is a type of Him who was to come. But the free gift is not like the transgression...For if by the transgression of the one, death reigned through the one, much more those who receive the abundance of grace and of the gift of righteousness will reign in life through the One, Jesus Christ. [Romans 5:12-15; 17]*

There it is, the case for original sin. Even if we, as individuals, had never sinned by our own thoughts, words or actions, we would still stand as guilty before the Lord because of the curse of sin upon all mankind. Because of Adam and Eve's disobedience back in the Garden of Eden, all of us are in need of a Savior. None of us can earn the salvation of our souls.

Besides, the sinful nature was passed down to us, as well, and so even if there were no original sin, we were doomed to fail. It might be hard to believe, but that is exactly what the Bible teaches. It says, *"the wages of sin is death"* and no one gets out of here alive.

So, there might be some logic that, just as with the lost coin, God put us in a position where sin was unavoidable. We didn't wander away totally on our own. That part of the story is true. But, it is also true that God gave us "free will," and we do have the ability (but maybe not the will) to resist sin. So, either way, whether we are more like the coin or the sheep, or a little of both, we cannot save ourselves. No one can. It doesn't matter if you have two billion dollars in the bank or if Billy Graham is your brother-in-law, money or human connections won't matter one bit (just another example of God's ways being very different from the ways of this world, where money and connections mean a lot).

Once again, only Jesus Christ who was sinless, Himself, has been given the power and authority, by the Father, to forgive us of our sins and restore us to our rightful place before God. And the offer has been given to everyone who has ever lived, so that all of us are without excuse. Let me repeat that, we have no legitimate excuse for not accepting Christ's invitation and forgiveness. None, nada, zip.

Take it from me, when Jesus said, in John Chapter 14, *"I am the way, and the truth, and the life; no one comes to the Father but through Me,"* He was as serious as a heart attack.

Contrary to what you may have heard, there is only one way to Heaven, Jesus Christ. He has purchased a ticket for you with His life and paid for it in full, with His own blood. Talk about "having skin in the game." No, Jesus does not wave a magic wand or just make promises. Rather, He took it upon Himself, to do the "heavy lifting."

Both the lost sheep and the lost coin were eventually found, and there was great rejoicing when they were. But they didn't find themselves. Can I get an "Amen?"

STORY THIRTY-TWO

"The Stakes Are Raised"

And He said, "A man had two sons. The younger of them said to his father, 'Father, give me the share of the estate that falls to me.' So, he divided his wealth between them. And not many days later, the younger son gathered everything together and went on a journey into a distant country, and there he squandered his estate with loose living. Now when he had spent everything, a severe famine occurred in that country, and he began to be impoverished. So, he went and hired himself out to one of the citizens of that country, and he sent him into his fields to feed swine. And he would have gladly filled his stomach with the pods that the swine were eating, and no one was giving anything to him. But when he came to his senses, he said, 'How many of my father's hired men have more than enough bread, but I am dying here with hunger! I will get up and go to my father, and will say to him, 'Father, I have sinned against heaven, and in your sight; I am no longer worthy to be called your son; make me as one of your hired men.' So, he got up and came to his father. But while he was still a long way off, his father saw him and felt compassion for him, and ran and embraced him and kissed him. And the son said to him, 'Father, I have sinned against heaven and in your sight; I am no longer worthy to be called your son.' But the father said to his slaves, 'Quickly bring out the best robe and put it on him, and put a ring on his hand and sandals on his feet; and bring the fattened calf, kill it, and let us eat and celebrate; for this son of mine was dead and has come to life again; he was lost and has been found.' And they began to celebrate." [Luke 15:11-24]

ZOOMING IN

And now, for the last episode of what I might call, "The Trilogy of Lost Things," we come to the longest parable we have talked about so far, and I have not even included the whole story in the quote above, for the sake of space and time. But we will talk about the whole story later, I assure you. In the first two episodes, we learned about lost sheep and lost coins, all things of value, I agree. But, now we are getting much more up close and personal, in this one. We are talking about a son. This is about a father and his own flesh and blood. Two sons, actually. You know the story, I'm sure. But let's dig a little deeper, if we can. If there is a parable that more accurately depicts the Gospel of Jesus Christ, I have not found it.

The parable of "The Prodigal Son" is probably, by far, the most beloved and certainly the most "referred to" parable that Jesus shared with us. There have been countless songs, books and movies all drawing from this incredible story of not only love, but heartache. Doesn't there always seem to be a connection between those two subjects? Love and heartache? That has been my experience. I suspect you would agree.

We have, here, a father who gives an inheritance to his two sons, both whom he loves dearly. It is interesting to note that it was the younger son who asked for his inheritance. That might have been a red flag moment. The other son was not worried about it, at that time, and that probably tells you all you need to know about the two sons. One was content to stay and wait for his time to come. The other one had, as they say, "money burning a hole in his pocket," and he had not even received it yet. But the father obliged and decided that if he was going to give it one son, he needed to be fair and give it to both of them. And so, he did.

Now, some might say that this father was lucky that both of his sons didn't "hit the road runnin' and let the good times roll." But, as we see a bit later, the older son did not. He stayed with his father, saved his inheritance and did everything that his father asked him to do, happy to serve until his time arrived and was also thankful for what the father had given him. Of course, all the younger son left behind was a cloud of dust. In no time at all, he was long gone, footloose and fancy free, with a ton of money in his traveling bag. And we are led to believe that he didn't deny himself much of anything, along the way. If he wanted it, he grabbed it...and he wanted it all.

As you might expect, even if you were not familiar with this story, the good times didn't last. A great famine came upon the land and it wasn't long until this young man found himself starving and broke, left to eat with the pigs, if you will. It is difficult, especially if you have not saved or prepared for the day of trouble, and it wasn't long until he started thinking about how good he had it at home with his father. In fact, he said to himself, "Even my father's servants are probably eating good, right about now. I would be better off to just be one of them."

So, he heads for home, with his tail between his legs, just hoping that his father might be willing to at least have mercy on him and let him just be as one of his servants. At that point, he knew how foolish he had been and was not expecting the royal treatment a son would receive. But he had underestimated the love of a good, good father. As we know, when the father sees him coming, he commands his servants to "roll out the red carpet," if you will. The father was so overjoyed that his son was coming home, he ran to him (no he didn't wait there with his arms folded, tapping his foot in anticipation, so he could give his rebellious son a well-deserved tongue lashing). He had considered him to be as good as dead and he was just thankful to have him back, safe and sound (albeit a bit bruised and broken).

Honestly, other than when our Heavenly Father spoke from Heaven saying of His Son, Jesus, ***"This is my beloved Son, in whom I am well-pleased," [Matthew 3:17]***, I cannot think of a more beautiful example of a father showing his unconditional love for a son ("unconditional" being the key word there).

If we learn nothing else from this story, I hope we all truly learn and never forget this one eternal truth. God loves you, no matter who you are or what you have done, more than you can ever imagine. And nothing you could ever do or say could ever lessen His love for you. It is absolutely unconditional, in the purest sense of the word.

Don't you ever doubt that for a single second.

ZOOMING OUT

So, as we close this final story from this group of things "Lost and Found," I do not want to overlook the good son in this story. What the father was willing to do for the "rebel without a cause" was truly astonishing, no doubt. And that is why this story is so loved and retold thousands of times. It just boggles the mind that any father, at least the earthly kind, could be that loving, that forgiving and that accepting of a son who basically trampled everything the father gave him under foot and treated it with total disrespect, as if somehow, he had earned it all himself. As far as we know from the story, this rebel didn't even say, "Thank you, father," either for the inheritance, in the first place, or the undeserved treatment he received upon returning home. It is almost too unbelievable to comprehend, is it not?

But, isn't it just like any great storyteller, to leave out that part of the story, as sort of a cliffhanger, to keep the listener thinking about it, saying, "I wonder how the story ended. Did the rebellious son stay home this time, or did he lick his wounds for a season and then run off again? We don't really know, do we? Maybe it's just as well.

But what about the other cliffhanger, the good son? What was his reward for all his good behavior? Did he receive more of an inheritance in the end? Was he promoted to a higher position in his father's estate? Was he singled out or recognized for his faithfulness and gratitude? Again, we are not sure, because Jesus doesn't elaborate too much on what happens later in this story.

But here is what we do know. This is what the father said to the good son, after he had raised some legitimate complaints:

'Son, you have always been with me, and all that is mine is yours. But we had to celebrate and rejoice, for this brother of yours was dead and has begun to live, and was lost and has been found.'" [Luke 15:31-32]

As far as we know, he was not given anything more than the rebellious son was given. But then again, if the father gives you all that he has, shares everything that is rightfully his, with you, just because you are indeed...A SON...nothing more and nothing less, what else is there to give? You have inherited everything. So, it is with our Father in Heaven.

Well, I don't mean to cut this story short, but we do have a wedding to prepare for!

PART FIVE

"Wedding Preparations"

"As many as you find there...
...invite to the wedding feast."

Matthew 22:9

STORY THIRTY-THREE

"Kids of the King"

I want to pause for a second, as we begin to delve into the fifth and final group of parables. I must say that I am not surprised to find, through my research for this book, that there definitely was an underlying story being woven into the "who, what, when and where" of these inspiring side stories that Jesus told. But, what I was surprised to find is just how clearly that larger story has revealed itself as we have progressed, step-by-step, through the study of the earthly ministry of our Lord Jesus and learned more about His kingdom, both as it was to be revealed here on Earth and how it will manifest in the hereafter.

What we are going to find, I think, in this last blast of stories is some (not all) of the answers to life's most nagging questions. Questions like, "Why are we here?" Or, "Why did God bother to create the Universe, in the first place?" And hopefully, "What does it all mean?" I won't be able to tell you, however, who is going to win the World Series or Super Bowl this year and I won't be able to say for sure just how many more sequels there will be in the "Fast and Furious" series. The Bible was curiously quiet on some things and didn't answer all of life's probing questions, but I digress.

Yes, God left some of it to be experienced, first-hand by us, the ones He created in His image. I'm guessing He wanted us to be able to feel the same sorrow or joy He feels when watching major events unfold in real time. Sometimes it is just better to see what happens with our own eyes, rather than being told what happened, right? But, I will give you a hint. The answers to most of those timeless questions generally can be boiled down to one word. Relationship.

To be more specific, I think the entirety of our existence, as humans, comes down to two things. First, realizing that Jesus has given us a "proposal of marriage," an offer to be united in an unending covenant relationship with Himself, and He has made all the necessary arrangements to make good on that proposal, should we accept His invitation.

And secondly, our time on this Earth is to be used to prepare ourselves for that glorious day, just as the bride prepares herself for her groom. If you have ever been around a "bride-to-be," good luck trying to get them to do anything except planning and making preparations for the wedding. And when they are not doing that, they are talking about it, right? And why not, it will be the biggest day of their entire life. Nothing else matters, at that moment.

Should our focus, with regards to our relationship with Christ, be any different. Eternity is a big deal. And as we will see, it begins with, what else, a marriage feast. Coincidence? I think not.

Meanwhile, the groom is off making the preparations for "what comes next," after the wedding. He is anxiously looking forward to, and making things ready for their life together beyond the wedding day and honeymoon. And, he is trying to make that part, also, the best it can possibly be.

After all, what good is being a king, if you have no kingdom to share it with?

ZOOMING IN

Then some children were brought to Him so that He might lay His hands on them and pray; and the disciples rebuked them. But Jesus said, "Let the children alone, and do not hinder them from coming to Me; for the kingdom of heaven belongs to such as these." [Matthew 19:13-14]

How fitting is it, then, that the very first parable we talk about in Part Five is primarily about children? What a great place to start. Is there anything more central to the concept of relationship than the miracle of being able to create little ones, just as God did, in our own image. And again, God did not just create us to be like Him physically (I talked about this at length in "Unlocking Creation"), but He made us like Himself emotionally and spiritually, as well.

He loves. We love. He laughs. We laugh. He weeps. We weep. He creates. We create. He expresses Himself and so do we, right? That may be the most puzzling thing, for me, when I talk to people who say they do not believe in God. Where do they think these traits and abilities came from? God gave us sight, hearing, taste, smell and touch. We did not develop those abilities on our own. God gave us intelligent minds that can reason and think and solve great problems. Can anyone teach themselves how to think? Oh sure, we can improve our minds through training and study. But the core functions, the basic impulses of the brain, were designed and built into us by a loving and gracious Creator. Did He not give us "free will?" Of course, He did, and in doing so, He knew some would use that power to reason Him out of the picture, so they could decide things for themselves, as Adam and Eve did. How'd that work out?

So yes, God gave us the ability to have children, or to **"be fruitful and multiply"** as it says in Genesis. The idea was that we would fill up the whole Earth with creatures made in God's image, people that have the ability to bring Him glory and bring Him joy. And again, knowing that not all His children would choose to do that, but we all are hard-wired with the ability to do so. Hang on to that point; it is an important one. I'll get back to that a bit later.

But before we do, I want to see if we can answer another one of life's enduring questions. One that is not that easy to answer for many of us, but I will try. Do children who die at an early age go to Heaven? And if so, at what age do they become responsible for their own actions and decisions?

We have all heard this talked about before, I'm sure. But, it is one matter I feel we need to dig a little deeper into, especially since it seems that the Master Storyteller has chosen to weigh in, Himself. It is always good to go right to the source, for answers, whenever possible, right? So, let's do that.

Jesus makes two very profound statements in this tiny little nugget of a parable, the first of which is:

"Let the children alone, and do not hinder them from coming to Me."

If I just take this at face value and don't try to get all "uber-spiritual" about it, what's not to understand? Jesus loves children and He does not want anyone or anything hindering or restricting them from coming to Him, physically or spiritually speaking, I presume. They are welcome, and He wants them to come. So, I am going out on a limb, here, to say I believe children are welcome in Heaven. He is basically saying, "Let 'em alone. Let them come to Me. It's not them I am concerned with. It's you guys, the older and smarter ones, that I have issues with." So, I am going to just leave it right there. Children go to Heaven, period.

But you may ask, "What about that 'original sin' stuff we talked about? Wouldn't that prevent them from going to Heaven, if it only takes one sin to disqualify us? My answer is, "No," and here's why. Some say it has to do with what they call "the age of accountability." But, is that age three, or ten, or thirty-three? That's just it. We all develop differently. So, I don't think a fixed age would work very well. Some children become more aware of certain things well before others do. Besides, God says, He looks at the heart.

I think God knows each of us, individually, well enough to know when we should be held accountable. He is a fair, just and merciful God. I trust He knows what's best in each situation. Works for me, who am I to question His judgment, anyway?

ZOOMING OUT

The second profound statement He made may take a little more explaining and fits in a little better with the bigger picture, so I thought we'd talk about it here:

"...for the kingdom of heaven belongs to such as these."

What could the Lord have meant by implying that the Kingdom of Heaven belongs to children? When we all are resurrected and go to be with Him in eternity, I know we all are supposed to get what they call a "glorified body." So, does this mean it will be the body of a five-year-old? Now that would be funny. Millions and millions of five-year-old kids running around like they have just been dropped off at Disney World. But, don't worry, there are no irritating noises in Heaven and you won't fall and scratch your knees or spill your ice cream cone two seconds after you get it, up there. It's Heaven. But, if we do have the body of five-year-old (not saying I believe that), I think it would be an interesting surprise for all the theologians, right? I can just see their faces, right now, probably covered in ice cream, as they wonder, "What happened? We did not see this one coming."

Simply put, Heaven is going to be amazing. No Satan, no sin, no temptation, no sickness and no death, not even the need for night or sleep. Only the glory of the living God and the light of His presence, forever and ever. Like the song says, "I can only imagine!!"

But honestly, when Jesus says the Kingdom belongs to **"such as these,"** I believe He is referring to people who are like children, specifically with regards to their innocence. These are people who are not driven by lust, power, money or their own egos.

As we get older, due to our sinful nature and the fact that we become more aware of the alternative choices at our fingertips, we become a lot more Adam and Eve-like and a lot less Christ-like. In other words, we start thinking that we are able to decide between right and wrong based on our own perceptions and values. That was the first couple's first mistake and it is often still ours today. We are constantly moving the goalposts around to where they best fit in with our agendas, to give ourselves the best chance of winning the trophy (whatever the trophy is we are seeking. . . the wife, the husband, the job, the promotion, the recognition or power, you name it). We kinda make the rules up as we go along, nowadays. Whatever feels good, do it!!

Little children are not like that. Life is much simpler for them. One day just blends into the next and they just know that someone will be there at the appropriate time, to provide whatever they need at any given moment. Whether it's food, clothes or whatever, it is not their job to worry about it. Oh yes, I know there are plenty of exceptions in this painful and sinful world we live in where the basic necessities of life are not always provided and that is heartbreaking to see, for sure. But generally speaking, kids just know they will be taken care of. And they usually are. I think that is what the Master Storyteller is talking about here. . . simple childlike faith.

So, in conclusion, yes, I do believe children go to Heaven and I believe the Lord knows when a child becomes accountable and when he or she is not quite there yet. I truly believe Jesus was speaking more about adults, in this parable, than the children. I believe He was saying that if we want to be with Him for all of eternity, it is not at all about a long list of "do's and don'ts," rules or regulations or even what church you attend. Rather, it is a matter of the heart.

It just comes down to having a simple childlike faith. If we believe there is a God in Heaven, then what on Earth is there to worry about? He's got the whole world in His hands....and that includes you and me. King Solomon said it this way:

Trust in the LORD with all your heart And do not lean on your own understanding.In all your ways acknowledge Him, And He will make your paths straight. [Proverbs 3:5-6]

Thank You, Father!!!

STORY THIRTY-FOUR

"The Willing and The Unwilling"

"But what do you think? A man had two sons, and he came to the first and said, 'Son, go work today in the vineyard.' And he answered, 'I will not'; but afterward he regretted it and went. The man came to the second and said the same thing; and he answered, 'I will, sir'; but he did not go. Which of the two did the will of his father?" They said, "The first." Jesus said to them, "Truly I say to you that the tax collectors and prostitutes will get into the kingdom of God before you. For John came to you in the way of righteousness and you did not believe him; but the tax collectors and prostitutes did believe him; and you, seeing this, did not even feel remorse afterward so as to believe him." [Matthew 21:28-32]

ZOOMING IN

Here we have another story about children, in fact another one involving two sons. And after reading this one, I can honestly say I think I understand why the Lord preferred young children. With the older ones, there seems to be too much thinking going on for my liking. It's not so much if they remember what you said, as it is with the little ones, but rather, do they choose to listen or obey? With the little ones, it is more likely they just forgot what they were told and they need more repetition to for it to sink in. It is called training.

With the grown-up ones, they know what is expected of them. They are just deciding if they want to comply or not. It's more of a "risk vs. reward" scenario with them. It's almost like they are saying, "What's in it for me, if I obey?" or, "What happens if I don't?"

I feel the need to tell a rather embarrassing story about myself, here, if you will indulge me for a moment. When I was in high school, during a summer break, my parents told me I had one job for the summer. We had a one-car garage, back then, and they just wanted me to paint the outside of it. Well, that didn't seem like too much to ask, and besides, they were giving me the whole summer to do it.

So, I decided to tackle it in small bites, rather than jumping on it and getting it done. But, of course, summer days have plenty of distractions and I got off to a really slow start, with most days coming and going without a single brush stroke. My dear mother, bless her heart, finally said, "How about if I help you and we can get it done sooner?" That sounded good. Anything to reduce the punishment (that is what it felt like to me. . . yeah. . . my parents went too easy one me, you're right?). Even still, with Mom being willing to chip in, I continued to procrastinate and after the first month, we only had one side done. And now, my summer was already slipping away, as football practice would be starting in a few weeks and we really would not get much done, once it did.

I'm guessing you probably have already figured out how the story ended. Mom ended up painting the rest herself and to be honest, I don't believe she ever told my Dad. If she had, I am sure the story would have ended much differently. But that was my Mom. She didn't want to get me in trouble. She definitely was too easy on me. And I am sorry to say, at age sixteen, I didn't know how good I had it. Well, I probably did, but I was not willing to let on that I did. I was quick to play the "I'm too busy" card or pull the "I'll do double tomorrow" bit (which I never did, of course). This speaks of relationships; someone usually does more than their share to make it work. And the other usually does less than their part. In this story, I was certainly "the other," I am sorry to say.

So back to the story at hand, we have two sons, here, and both were told to go work in the father's field. One said, "Sorry, no can do." The other said, "You got it, sir." This is a great example of why it is never a good idea to judge a story by how it starts. If you did, with this one, the second son would clearly be the "good guy." No hesitation, he just says, "I'll do it." No questions asked. No excuses given.

But as the story unfolds, we see that although the first one said, "No," at first, he ended up reconsidering and did show up for work. He must have done the whole, "risk vs. reward" thing and decided it was going to be worse for him down the road, if he didn't show up.

The second one, on the other hand, said, "No problem" initially, but then procrastinated and never showed up. As much as I hate to admit it now, this is the category I would have fit into with the garage story. I said, "Sure, sounds reasonable. I'd be happy to." But, I managed to wiggle out of it and leave it on dear old Mom's disappointed shoulders. What a guy, huh? I know. I hear ya.

What strikes me the most about this parable is the fact that the Master Storyteller asks them which son did the will of the father. They replied, "The first one." But Jesus does not actually say if they answered correctly or not. It appears that the right answer might have been "none of the above." It does seem to make sense that the first son eventually complied, as if to say, "Better late than never." But just based on what is written here in the Scriptures, it seems Jesus was looking for a different answer (and no, it was not the second son).

ZOOMING OUT

To find the "big picture" take on this one, we need to first remember who Jesus was speaking to in this story. He was in the Temple, in Jerusalem, and He was answering some of the questions from the chief priests and elders who, again, were trying to trap Him. As best as I can tell, the true answer came at the end, in verse thirty-two. Let's take another look:

"For John came to you in the way of righteousness and you did not believe him; but the tax collectors and prostitutes did believe him; and you, seeing this, did not even feel remorse afterward so as to believe him." [Matthew 21:32]

So, it appears the right answer was, in fact, neither. The very last part, there, says it all. He tells them, *"and you did not even feel remorse afterward so as to believe him."* It was true that the first son did not agree to go to work at first, as the second son did. But when Jesus pointed His answer at the Jews, He was basically saying to them: *While it is true, you did not believe at first when John came to you, but as with the first son, you showed no remorse afterwards. You did not start well, nor did you end well. You failed to heed the call at all. And that is worse than either of the sons in the story.*

I believe it is fair to say that Jesus was not increasing the size of His fan club with this story, especially when they realized He was pointing it directly at them. Not all, and it was not going to be too much longer until they made the decision to silence this troublemaker, once and for all. The clock was ticking.

So, what are we to make of this story? Is there a moral, here, for us to learn from?

The first son went to work, but not right away. The second son intended to go, but he did not. And neither of these guys got any "brownie points" from the Master Storyteller. It seemed He was focused in on a totally different part of the equation. Remorse.

Jesus, as we talked about earlier, was all about repentance and redemption. He was always talking about turning from sin and seeking God. For that to happen, a person needs to come to grips with that fact that they have something be sorry for. I eventually came to the place where I felt sorry about leaving my sweet, loving mother with the painting of that garage, but much too late I'm afraid. So sorry, Mom!! Yet, there was eventually remorse.

You see, although the first son ended up going to work, we have no idea if he did it for the right reasons. He may just have realized it was going to cost him in the future. That is not really remorse. That is minimizing the bleeding. The second son had good intentions, but wiggled out of it and we have no evidence that he ever felt bad about it. Again, there was no sign of remorse.

To put this into a setting that fits in with Part Five here, "Wedding Preparations," have you ever known anyone who got married for the wrong reasons? Money, status, looks or whatever? How did that work out? Occasionally, it does, but not all that often.

On the other side of the coin, have you ever known anyone who said, "Yes," but then go cold feet and couldn't go through with it? This scenario usually works out a little better, only because some might say, "We are better off. If we had married, it would not have ended well." So yes, I think it's better to say, "I'll marry you," and then wimp out for the right reasons, then to say no to marriage and eventually cave in and get married for the wrong reasons. But, wouldn't you agree, neither is the ideal situation? I believe that is the essence of what the Lord was saying in this story.

Marriage is a covenant relationship. It is a lifelong commitment. It is not something you try for a year or two and see how it goes (although based on the trends for marriage and divorce, these days, some might disagree with me). You should never get married for the wrong reasons. Love, true love, the kind that lasts a lifetime should be the only reason to get hitched.

There is an old saying (and I'm old enough to remember it) that says, "If you can't say, "Forever," don't say, "I do.""

I believe the same thing is true with our eternal relationship with God, through Jesus Christ. As we have learned, He referred to Himself as "the Bridegroom." We are the ones who must decide whether to accept His proposal of "happily ever after" or not. But we should only accept His proposal for the right reasons. If we say, "Well, Hell sounds like a nasty place. I need fire insurance," or "Heaven sounds fantastic. Count me in," those are not the right reasons.

King David was referred to as "a man after God's heart." He was also a man who screwed up royally, pardon the pun. If any man felt real remorse, David did. As the writer of the Psalms, he went to great lengths to let God know just how sorry and remorseful he was about his sins. Here is one of his most famous responses:

The sacrifices of God are a broken spirit; A broken and a contrite heart, O God, You will not despise. [Psalm 51:17]

Not offerings or sacrifices, he said. What God loved was David's broken and contrite heart. Remorse. And that is really all that God wants from us. God knows we are all sinners, it says so right in the Bible. But He is looking for the ones who realize the full weight of their sin and are ready to not just admit it, but also, turn from it. Because you see, real remorse produces repentance.

It's not so much that God takes pleasure in making us feel miserable. That's not it at all. But He realizes that if we don't truly feel the weight of our sin, we won't likely seek to get out from under it.

We might say we want to, but like the second son in our story, those feelings won't last.

God wants us to be joined to His Son for the right reasons, or not at all. He agreed to die for us, for the right reason. LOVE.

Does that make sense?

STORY THIRTY-FIVE

"Proper Dress Required"

Jesus spoke to them again in parables, saying, "The kingdom of heaven may be compared to a king who gave a wedding feast for his son. And he sent out his slaves to call those who had been invited to the wedding feast, and they were unwilling to come. Again, he sent out other slaves saying, 'Tell those who have been invited, "Behold, I have prepared my dinner; my oxen and my fattened livestock are all butchered and everything is ready; come to the wedding feast."' But they paid no attention and went their way, one to his own farm, another to his business, and the rest seized his slaves and mistreated them and killed them. But the king was enraged, and he sent his armies and destroyed those murderers and set their city on fire. Then he said to his slaves, 'The wedding is ready, but those who were invited were not worthy. Go therefore to the main highways, and as many as you find there, invite to the wedding feast.' Those slaves went out into the streets and gathered together all they found, both evil and good; and the wedding hall was filled with dinner guests.

"But when the king came in to look over the dinner guests, he saw a man there who was not dressed in wedding clothes, and he said to him, 'Friend, how did you come in here without wedding clothes?' And the man was speechless. Then the king said to the servants, 'Bind him hand and foot, and throw him into the outer darkness; in that place there will be weeping and gnashing of teeth.' For many are called, but few are chosen." [Matthew 22:1-14]

ZOOMING IN

So, I decided to call Part Five of this book "Wedding Preparations" because that is mainly what this last grouping of parables is about. Everything that we talked about, so far, in this book and everything we will yet talk about here is leading up to something quite spectacular, a wedding unlike any this world has ever known, which is quite fitting because the wedding feast I am talking about is truly "out of this world," literally.

I don't know how many you have ever read or heard about traditional Jewish wedding customs, but I think it would be very helpful, at this point, to take a brief look at some of them to give us a proper point of reference for what Jesus is talking about. Let's not forget, Jesus was a Jew and His earthly ministry was started at, of course, a Jewish wedding. You might think our wedding celebrations are a big deal nowadays (and they are). Well, the Jews took it to a whole 'nother level and then some.

I know I'm curious. How about you? Just, keep in mind, every little detail has a symbolic importance, related in one way or another, to the "granddaddy of all weddings" that is yet to come.

And as I said, this is just a brief overview. I would highly recommend looking online at a fuller description of the traditions. It is eye-opening, to say the least:

1.   A wedding may not be held on a Sabbath, during any of the seven Jewish Feasts, during the three weeks set aside to commemorate the destruction of the Temple, or during the seven weeks between Passover and Shavuot (Pentecost), which when added together is over half of the year. Oh, and if someone in the immediate family is in mourning at the time the wedding is scheduled, they had to postpone it for at least thirty days. Ouch!! And we think we have a hard time setting a date or finding a hall.

2.   A Ketuba (a marriage contract), which outlines the bridegroom's responsibilities towards the bride, is signed and an appropriate amount for a dowry is set. It also includes a written obligation that the bride is to receive the groom's full estate and possessions, if he should die. Sounds like a prenuptial agreement and a will, sort of all rolled into one. This tradition still continues

today, but it has no real legal significance. It is just between them and God. Interesting, huh?

3.   Before the ceremony, the Rabbi, the two fathers, the bridegroom and his attendants enter the bride's chamber (what?) for what is called the badekan (veiling) ceremony. This points to when Jacob worked for seven years to earn the right to marry Rachel, only to have her father substitute Leah, instead. Okay, that one made me chuckle, too, but remember it is all about tradition. That is hugely important in all of this. Now, in our weddings, the groom is prohibited from seeing the bride on the day of the wedding, before the ceremony. They say it is "bad luck." But could it really be so they can secretly switch out the bride, if they choose to? Just askin." Okay, yes, I am making a little joke. But it cost Jacob another seven years of work, just to be able to marry the girl of his dreams. That was not funny.

4.   As soon as the ceremony has ended, there is no "receiving line," as we do nowadays, there is a time of seclusion (10-20 minutes) called the Yichud for the bride and groom to be alone with each other. Some say, if the bride and groom had been fasting before the ceremony, this is a time where they can break the fast. Others say it is a time for them to consummate their marriage and make it official. I'll let you decide which one you think is right. What happens most of the time now, in non-Jewish weddings, is the bride, the groom and the wedding party disappear for a while to take professional pictures to commemorate the day's events. Hey, gotta have pictures, right?'. There's Facebook, Twitter, Instagram, Snapchat, c'mon. How else are we going to tell the world?

5.   Last but not least, is the appropriate wedding attire, which of course is white to symbolize pureness, since a wedding is considered a personal Yom Kippur for the couple. It is a time of repentance (change and direction) and forgiveness (fresh start) for them, as well. The bride and groom have prepared themselves properly for this day and it's important to start off with a clean slate and the blessings of God to be able to face what lies ahead.

Well, there you have it, a bird's eye view of the Jewish wedding traditions and what they symbolize. I hope you found that as interesting as I did, when compared to the way most folks approach it today. (Night and day, to say the least). But trust me, as we are approaching the end of the greater story being told by Jesus, here, all of this will matter, big time., So thanks for allowing me to wander seemingly off-track, here for a bit. Like the Master Storyteller, I am laying the groundwork for what is to come.

One more interesting tradition is that a traditional Jewish wedding invitation does not include the words, "request the honor of your presence," but rather to "dance at" or "share in the joy of." Guests at Jewish wedding were not "doing you a favor" by being there or honoring the couple with their presence. No, they were just happy to be invited. Thrilled, actually. To not be invited, now that would have been very troubling, or in some cases, even embarrassing. It is also interesting, that in the listing of traditions I read, there was no mention of the need for the invitee to RSVP. I guess, if you were invited, it was not considered likely that you would refuse. Again. . .think tradition here. What did the Jews do, when Jesus arrived? Did they humbly and graciously accept His invitation? We know the answer to that question, all too well, I'm afraid.

So now, let's take another look at the story we are supposed to be talking about in this chapter. I think we might be able to better see where Jesus was going, now that we know the back-story. The father is preparing this great wedding feast. He invites the desired guests, not once, but twice. They ignore and refuse the invitation both times. The father is not happy about this, so he tells his servants to go out and invite "as many as you find there," basically "everyone else."

Keep in mind, the ones who were invited first and refused, they paid dearly for their disrespect (only a few short years after Jesus came to them and was rejected, the Temple was destroyed by the Romans and the Jews were exiled from their land for two thousand years). Coincidence? I think not. So, the Gospel message, then, was sent forth to the Gentiles, to the whole world, in fact. And as the Apostle Paul says in Romans 11, God basically invited us just to make the Jews jealous or show them what they missed:

I say then, they (the Jews) did not stumble so as to fall, did they? May it never be! But by their transgression salvation has come to the Gentiles, to make them jealous. [Romans 11:11]

That is not to say we, as Gentiles, were afterthoughts. No, God had every intention of offering redemption to all His children. Yet, in extending the invitation to us, God was still being redemptive towards Israel, not spiteful. He wanted them to reconsider and be remorseful (like the first son in our last discussion). He wanted them to turn back to Him and finally accept His invitation.

Always remember, God is faithful, He keeps His promises and His love is unconditional. He didn't revoke His invitation to the Jews, in this story. No, He just invited everyone else. He left the door open for them to have a change of heart.

How incredible is that?

ZOOMING OUT

Let's take a brief look at the end of this parable, if we can, I think it is equally important:

"But when the king came in to look over the dinner guests, he saw a man there who was not dressed in wedding clothes, and he said to him, 'Friend, how did you come in here without wedding clothes?' And the man was speechless...For many are called, but few are chosen." [Matthew 22:11-12;14]

What is the Lord talking about here, regarding "wedding clothes?" Earlier, we talked about wedding attire being white (the bride and groom, of course) and the symbolism of a wedding being about pureness, repentance and forgiveness. . . as with Yom Kippur.

Did not Jesus refer to Himself as the Bridegroom? Is the Church not referred to in the Scriptures as His Bride? Are we not, then, just as a bride does before a wedding, to prepare for that day, to make ourselves pure and clean and fit to meet the Bridegroom when that glorious and long-awaited day arrives?

Of course we are, but how are we to make ourselves clean, pure, and suitable to be joined to Him. Let's look at one more Jewish wedding tradition. Before the wedding, the bride was to go to the Temple for the "mikvah," which was like a large bathtub, similar to the baptismals we see in a lot of churches today. She was to undergo "full immersion" (again like Christian baptism. . . Catholics and some other churches do this differently, of course) to symbolize purity and that she has adequately prepared herself for the ceremony.

And we also know, that the Bible speaks about believers being "washed in the blood" for the forgiveness of sin and that Christ's blood was shed to provide payment for the forgiveness of sin. Back in the first chapter of this book, Jesus turned the water into wine. Later, He would say we are to take a cup of wine and drink from it, that it symbolized His blood being shed. Water became wine. Wine symbolizes blood. And blood equals forgiveness. Are we seeing the connection there? The Prophet Isaiah explained it this way:

"Come now, and let us reason together," says the Lord. "Though your sins are as scarlet, they will be as white as snow; Though they are red like crimson, they will be like wool." [Isaiah 1:18]

Without forgiveness, our sins are as scarlet in the eyes of God. And only the blood of the Lamb can make them "white as snow."

But first, you need to accept the invitation. The Bridegroom has proposed and everyone has been invited. Are you going to accept and put on the proper wedding clothes, that being Christ, of course? That decision is up to you and no one else.

Like it says, "Many are called, but few are chosen." Not everyone is going to accept the Bridegroom's invitation. In fact, we are led to believe that most will not. This is very sad.

Hope 2 C Ya There!!

STORY THIRTY-SIX

"Looking for Figs"

"Now learn the parable from the fig tree: when its branch has already become tender and puts forth its leaves, you know that summer is near; so, you too, when you see all these things, recognize that He is near, right at the door. Truly I say to you, this generation will not pass away until all these things take place. Heaven and earth will pass away, but My words will not pass away. But of that day and hour no one knows, not even the angels of heaven, nor the Son, but the Father alone. For the coming of the Son of Man will be just like the days of Noah."
[Matthew 24:32-37]

ZOOMING IN

Public confession time, here, I have greatly enjoyed digging into each and every one of the side stories we have talked about so far, without a doubt. But I have been looking forward with great anticipation to unpacking this one, and the next one as well, since they deal with a subject I have a great deal of interest in and passion about (for obvious reasons), the Second Coming of Jesus Christ. And in this chapter, we have Jesus, Himself, talking just to His twelve Disciples, not a bunch of naysayers who are out to get Him. So, it is safe to assume that Jesus felt comfortable "opening up" about these things with this group of men, for two reasons.

First, since they asked Him, He wanted to be as frank and revealing as possible, since they were the ones who would be carrying on in His place and would likely have a lot explaining to do, once He was gone. And secondly, they were beginning to realize He was not going to be with them much longer and that He was promising to return again, at some point. So obviously, they wanted to know what signs to look for that would alert them that His return was imminent.

At this point, they did not know if He would be gone for a week, two months or two thousand years. They wanted to stay ready, because He hinted that He could come back at any time, like a flash of lightning or a thief in the night. They were not about to miss that and they were hoping for some advance warning, if possible, so they could alert as many people as possible. So, they asked Him, *"Tell us, when will these things happen?" [Matthew 24:3]*

What is interesting about how Jesus chose to answer their question, is how He used the illustration of a fig tree. He had already cursed a fig tree for not bearing fruit and there was another parable, one we talked about earlier, where the owner wanted to chop one down because he had not seen any fruit for two years. Remember, his servant asked if he could be given another year to see if he could bring it around. In each of these instances, many Bible experts believe that the fig tree was symbolic of Israel and that Jesus was pointing to the fact that they had not produced fruit (hold onto that thought, I will elaborate a bit later).

I have to be honest here, before I became a Christian and started studying the Bible, my knowledge of figs was limited to one of my favorite cookies as a child, Fig Newtons. So, seeing how often Jesus talked about fig trees was quite surprising to me. But, now that I have learned He was using it to symbolize Israel, it all makes perfect sense.

So, yes, Jesus was telling His Disciples that a fig tree, or Israel, would bloom again (apparently after not blooming for a while) and that would be a major sign that His return was near. First of all, why would this fig tree not have been in bloom for a long time? What had happened? Jesus knew what was coming, but His Disciples did not. It would only be about forty years later, after He would die on a cross, be raised from the dead and ascend back into Heaven, that Jerusalem would be destroyed by the Romans in 70AD and the Jews would be exiled, not to return to their homeland for about two thousand years. Yes, they paid dearly for ignoring His arrival as Messiah and rejecting the Good News of salvation that He offered.

He also went on to say, that when it did finally bloom again, it would mark the beginning of the last generation before He returns to gather His people, just as He had promised to do. And the Master Storyteller also knew, as we have discussed before, that these twelve men were not the only ones who would get to hear or read His explanation. He knew His words would be written down and be permanently saved in a book called the Bible, for generations to come, so we could know the signs, as well.

Well, guess what? Fast forward to modern times, when Israel became a nation again on May 14th, 1948, every Bible scholar on Earth knew that something miraculous had just happened, something greater than anything that had happened in two thousand years. The fig tree had just come back into bloom and, if the Bible was correct, the last generation had officially begun. Many had said that was the one Biblical prophecy that would never be fulfilled. They did not believe it would ever happen; yet by God's grace, it did. God kept His promise to Israel, again.

Is it any wonder, then, that there has been this huge upswing in books, TV shows, movies and, need I say it, sermons regarding the Final Days before Christ's return and what it all means for the people of Earth today, believers and unbelievers alike. I know I'm not surprised, although I am a little surprised that even more people aren't talking about it. I mean, if we are living in the last generation of the world as we know it, shouldn't we be more focused on getting ready for His arrival and spreading the Good News to as many people as we can, since it could come at any moment?

"Therefore be on the alert, for you do not know which day your Lord is coming...For this reason you also must be ready; for the Son of Man is coming at an hour when you do not think He will." [Matthew 24:42,44]

Isn't that the reason that the bus lines and airlines publish their schedules ahead of time? They want people to know that a bus or a plane will be available to take them wherever they want to go. But, they also need to know that they have to show up, be packed and ready to go when it arrives, or they will miss it. FYI, this departure that Jesus is referring to, none of us should be willing to miss. There is not another bus coming in twenty minutes, an hour later or how about, never.

The Master Storyteller was telling them to keep a watchful eye out for figs. When they did show up, it would be time to get ready for departure. Well, that allegorical tree finally bloomed again about seventy years ago, and I don't know about you, but my experience tells me a generation is not much longer than seventy years. So, we might have maybe another ten or twenty years or so, if that, providing the Bible experts are correct. If you want my humble opinion, we are way passed the point where we should begin to get ready. We should already be ready. What is that old saying again? Oh yeah, "He who hesitates is lost." I'd say that certainly applies here.

ZOOMING OUT

But of that day and hour no one knows, not even the angels of heaven, nor the Son, but the Father alone. For the coming of the Son of Man will be just like the days of Noah." *[Matthew 24:36-37]*

No, you are not experiencing "déjà vu," I did share this same verse back in "Figless." But, like the Master Storyteller, I want to look at it again, but from a slightly different angle. The last time we looked at it as a time-keeping issue. This time, I want to look at it as more of a social commentary. Here, Jesus reflects on the story of Noah and the Ark, by saying that those days would be very similar to the days in which He will return to the Earth. One might be tempted to say, "How so, Lord?" I know I was, when I first saw this.

Well, as the story goes, those days were exceedingly evil. And in addition, He said people were ***"eating and drinking, marrying and giving in marriage. . ."*** (vs. 38) (there it is, again, a reference to marriage). They weren't really concerning themselves with God or impending judgment. But God had made it clear to Noah that a great flood was coming and that he was to begin to prepare, by building a boat large enough to preserve the lives of himself, his wife, their three sons and their wives, plus two of each variety of animal to make sure they would all be able to survive the flood and repopulate the Earth. Everyone else would not survive. God was basically hitting the restart button on humanity, because it had become so evil and self-consumed.

Would you say, by looking around at the world today, that we may be in similar times? Would you say we have largely become more concerned with ourselves and our own well-being, rather than looking to God and looking out for the needs others? I would.

When you stir that into the mix with what Jesus said about the fig tree coming back into bloom and Israel once again becoming a nation in 1948, wouldn't it be reasonable to assume that the day of the Lord's return is probably closer than we think? My guess is, absolutely. Sure, it is just a guess. I do not in believe setting dates. But Jesus said we should recognize the seasons and take note of the signs.

Earlier in this chapter, I talked about the fact that Jesus was suggesting that Israel, or the fig tree, had not produced fruit. So, what does that mean? What was He pointing to? Well, I will talk about this at length, in an upcoming chapter, I promise. But I do want to give you a hint, since it so important to our own "getting ready" and "bearing fruit."

In John 15, Jesus refers to Himself as the vine and His father being the vinedresser. He is saying to bear fruit, we must be "in Him," meaning Christ. Israel, up until that time anyway, had not recognized Jesus as God, as the Messiah. They didn't not accept the wedding invitation. But, as I said, the door was not closed to them. There was still hope. Still, they had not produced eternal fruit, because they were not "in Christ." In fact, they were the ones who were about to be pruned. But they didn't have a clue.

Let's hear it from Jesus, Himself:

"I am the true vine, and My Father is the vinedresser. Every branch in Me that does not bear fruit, He takes away; and

every branch that bears fruit, He prunes it so that it may bear more fruit....I am the vine, you are the branches; he who abides in Me and I in him, he bears much fruit, for apart from Me you can do nothing." [John 15:1-2,5]

My takeaway is that being connected to the vine and being "in Him" is synonymous and that it all is symbolic, somehow, of a marriage relationship. There definitely seems to be a connection there.

We shall see.

STORY THIRTY-SEVEN

"Regarding Lamps and Oil"

"Then the kingdom of heaven will be comparable to ten virgins, who took their lamps and went out to meet the bridegroom. Five of them were foolish, and five were prudent. For when the foolish took their lamps, they took no oil with them, but the prudent took oil in flasks along with their lamps. Now while the bridegroom was delaying, they all got drowsy and began to sleep. But at midnight there was a shout, 'Behold, the bridegroom! Come out to meet him.' Then all those virgins rose and trimmed their lamps. The foolish said to the prudent, 'Give us some of your oil, for our lamps are going out.' But the prudent answered, 'No, there will not be enough for us and you too; go instead to the dealers and buy some for yourselves.' And while they were going away to make the purchase, the bridegroom came, and those who were ready went in with him to the wedding feast; and the door was shut. Later the other virgins also came, saying, 'Lord, lord, open up for us.' But he answered, 'Truly I say to you, I do not know you.' Be on the alert then, for you do not know the day nor the hour." [Matthew 25:1-13]

ZOOMING IN

This particular side story that Jesus told His Disciples has special significance for me, as it was really the first one of His parables that I really got a firm grip on when I first came to Christ back in 1979. And of course, because I have been a musician most of my life, it was through an amazing song called "Sorry," written and recorded by a fellow Northeast Ohio musician and world class guitarist, Phil Keaggy, that this thought-provoking illustration came to life for me. As a new believer and long-time musician, I was getting a lot of my spiritual food through Christian music, which was very prolific in those days. The so-called "Jesus Movement" had opened the door to all these amazing songwriters and singers (like Keith Green, Second Chapter of Acts, Sweet Comfort Band, Love Song, Amy Grant, Michael W. Smith, Phil Keaggy and many others) to start writing and singing about the love of God and the Gospel of Jesus Christ. And trust me, I learned a lot from these songs and songwriters and I still often go back and listen to those songs to this day. Some of those lyrics were amazing, back then.

Phil's song about this very revealing parable was one of those. It painted this beautiful picture of ten virgins awaiting the return of the bridegroom, trying to stay ready, but five had not made sure to have enough oil on hand to keep their lamps lit. When it gets to the part where Jesus says to the five foolish ones, "I never knew you," you will sense the full gravity of this powerful story; I have no doubt. I would highly recommend you go to YouTube and search for the song "Sorry" by Phil Keaggy. Trust me, this parable will come to life for you in a new and inspiring way. He is an amazing songwriter, singer and musician.

But, the story told in both this parable and the song brings me to another Jewish wedding tradition, one that maybe sets the tone for the Gospel of Jesus Christ, as a whole, better than all the others. Maybe that is why this parable has always been one of my favorites.

You see, what we call an engagement, the Jews called the betrothal. It involved the groom travelling from his father's house, to the home of the prospective bride (no matter how far that was), where he would ask the father for her hand in marriage, pay the dowry (called the mohar), and establish the marriage agreement we talked about. Once that was all properly done and accepted, he would return to his own father's house for a year to prepare a place, a dwelling for the bride and groom to live in, once the wedding feast was completed. The bride, during that time was to prepare herself for this blessed event and "keep her lamp lit," because she did not know the day and hour which the bridegroom would return.

Are the dots starting to connect here? I'm serious, this parable is extremely content rich. I could probably spend the rest of this book and then some, just talking about all the spiritual lessons that are in this one little story that Jesus told His Disciples. One more side note, here, I found it very interesting that Jesus told this story to His Disciples, a bunch of men. None of them would ever be brides. None of them would ever have to "keep their lamps lit" while they awaited the return of a bridegroom. Or would they?

That is why this is a parable. It is not really about ten virgins at all. That is just an illustration the Master Storyteller is using to make a larger point. So, what could that larger point be? And why an illustration about a coming marriage and a betrothal? Trust me, He is going somewhere with all these marriage references. This is not just random ramblings, here. Jesus has a precise destination in mind and it is only now, little by little, that it is coming into view.

For the sake of our discussion, I will refrain from getting too long-winded on this and just give you the cream of the crop, here. The headline of it all would have to be "Stay Ready." But there are few other key issues that we need to touch on, since there is going to be this wedding feast that tops all other wedding feasts at some point in the future, and we do not want to miss out on a technicality, do we? Of course not.

When it comes to earthly marriages, we all know, ideally, we are meant to remain pure until the day comes when we are joined to the one that will be our "better half" for the rest of our lives. We are to save ourselves for them. I think it's fair to say that prerequisite has gone the way of the Hula-Hoop and the Pony Express in our modern society. But, let's just say that the use of the word "virgins," in this parable, was to imply that we all should be pure, or in other words, sinless.

I think that is a fair interpretation. But, we know that none of us, even from our birth, are sinless. Certainly, Jesus was aware of that. So how are we to overcome that obstacle? How does someone who is not capable of being ready or pure, in that way, become "ready?" The answer, of course, is that the debt of our sin would have to be somehow cancelled or removed. The word "forgiveness" leaps to mind and the picture of the Cross would loom large in providing the method by which that remedy could be applied. Because, once we are "in Christ," we are forgiven and God no longer sees our sin. He only sees Jesus in us.

Secondly, once the bride makes herself ready, the next thing to tackle was the problem of staying ready until the groom would return and only God knows when that would be. For me, the illustration of a lit lamp and the need for plenty of oil paints a pretty clear picture of what Jesus may have meant by that. Let me share another verse, here, that may help clarify it a bit further:

"If you then, being evil, know how to give good gifts to your children, how much more will your heavenly Father give the Holy Spirit to those who ask Him?" [Luke 11:13]

So, Jesus is saying the Father gives those who ask, the Holy Spirit. And wouldn't you know it, oil is often believed to be symbolic of the Holy Spirit in the Bible. But, how much will He give us? Apparently, the more we ask for it, the more He gives us. So, we should never run out of oil. If we do, it's our fault, not His.

In this one little side story about ten virgins waiting for a soon returning bridegroom, we see the need to be "made ready," which can only come through Jesus Christ. And, we learn that God also gives us a Helper, to help keep us ready. Oil for our lamps. And the oil that the Father gives us is none other than the Holy Spirit, which He gives to all believers when we come to Christ and ask to be forgiven.

Remember the conversation between Nicodemus and Jesus? He told him about being "born of the Spirit." This is what He was talking about. The "new birth," or second birth (as some call it). We are all are born of the water (physically). And to become spiritually alive, we need to be born of the Spirit.

"God is spirit, and those who worship Him must worship in spirit and truth." [John 4:24]

But there still is one other major factor to consider from this parable. When will the Bridegroom return?

ZOOMING OUT

Now while the bridegroom was delaying, they all got drowsy and began to sleep. But at midnight there was a shout, 'Behold, the bridegroom! Come out to meet him.' Then all those virgins rose and trimmed their lamps. [Matthew 25:5-7]

Well, tradition tells us it is a year until the bridegroom returns. But from the parable, it seems they did not know exactly when Jesus would come back. And to make matters worse, they fell asleep. Jesus addresses both problems at the end of the parable. *Be on the alert then, for you do not know the day nor the hour."* */v 13/* Repetition, my friends, repetition. We hear this theme over and over again, and let's face it, the Jews, all through history, had no idea of when the Messiah was going to come. If they did, they would not have missed it.

But the other key that our Master Storyteller tosses out there, is the fact that the groom in the story came when? At midnight. He came when it was dark. He came at a time when they needed a lamp, filled with oil and trimmed, to be able to see their beloved coming back for them. I believe that is how it will be with the return of Christ. He will come at a time of utter darkness. He will come at a time when people will need help to see Him, in the midst of that darkness.

Yes, the Bible says, "every eye will see Him," when He comes again. It will be unmistakable this time around. I do believe every single human being on the face of the Earth will see His arrival. With the advent of television, computers, smart phones and 24/7 cable news programs, oh yeah, we will all see it happen. No doubt.

But, not everyone will see Him for who He truly is. Only those whose lamps have been made ready, who have been forgiven and made pure in His eyes. And, only those whose lamps are full of the oil, born of the Spirit, only they will see Him in the fullness of His glory.

You think "Blue Ray" or "4K TV" is incredible? You ain't seen nothin' yet!!!

parable, here. I am going to give you my take on it. You may agree or disagree, but either way it's all good. I always say, "If we aren't talking, we aren't learning."

So, in this parable, Jesus is telling the Disciples that they are going to experience grief once He is taken from them, and the world will rejoice in it. But that it will only be temporary. There will come a time when their grief will be turned to joy and their weeping to rejoicing. That, I believe, was not only true for the Disciples, but for us as well.

Remember, Jesus being the living Word of God, knew He was not just talking to His Disciples. He knew His words would be seen and heard for generations to come and that even those who would be alive in the Final Days before His return, they would likely have the same questions. So, I believe what applied to them, back then, applies to us today.

He is telling them, as with a woman who is in labor and experiences a great deal of travail and agony right before and leading up to the blessed day, that they were going to go through some heartache after He was gone. But, when they are finally "born out of this world" and into eternity, they will be so happy and filled with joy, they won't even remember the pain. I know that is the hope that I hang onto with all my might. The things of this life are not always easy, but I know that glorious day is coming when I will be free of this world and it's struggles and grief. Hallelujah and Maranatha (which means "Come, O Lord").

So, hear me out, if you will, this is where I am at odds with the idea of a Pre-Tribulation Rapture, as it is taught so often these days.

I do not see any evidence that Jesus ascribed to that way of thinking. He certainly didn't avoid the hard stuff and I'm pretty sure the Disciples didn't believe that way, either, as all but one of them (John) were martyred for their faith in Christ. I'm sure they would have all gladly opted for leaving this world that way, without all the pain and suffering, had they been given that option.

But, Jesus told them that they would suffer for His namesake. It goes with the territory. The Apostle Paul likewise said, *"I do share on behalf of His body, which is the church...in Christ's afflictions." [Colossians 1:24]* Ask Paul if it would be all right for the Gentiles to be redeemed and taken home to be with the Lord before the Jews. Ask him if he thought it would be fitting for us to be spared tribulation, and not them. I don't think we would like his answer.

Jesus, Himself, near the end of this "Farewell Discourse," said the following words as He was praying to His Father, *"I do not ask You to take them out of the world, but to keep them from the evil one." [John 17:15]* So, I guess what I am zeroing in on, is that God does not have to take us "out of the world," as in a Pre-Trib Rapture, to protect us from the evil one.

Yes, I do believe there will be a day when Jesus returns and in the blink of an eye, all who are dead in Christ will rise first and meet Him in the air and we will follow quickly thereafter. But, God did not have to remove Noah and his family from the Earth, to protect them from the flood. Rather, He provided a way for them to be preserved through it. So, for me, it is not so much about "Is there a rapture or not?" It's more about when this "catching away" will occur.

I hope you see my heart, here. I just have a hard time grasping the idea of the New Testament Church, somehow being plucked from this world before things get bad, when the Jews would be left behind to suffer terribly. Are we not all one tree, now? Have we not been grafted in? If so, why would God choose to call us home, and not His chosen people, Israel?

Isn't this woman that Jesus speaks of in travail? Isn't it at the end of the ordeal that she no longer remembers the pain? At this point, the real contractions had not kicked in yet. Jesus was only talking about the birth pangs. Right after that He says, *"Then they will deliver you to tribulation,"* and, *"But the one who endures to the end, he will be saved." [Matthew 24:9; 13]* It is at the end of the travail that the joy comes, in my opinion, not in the middle of it all. My wife gave birth to four beautiful children and I'm pretty sure that she was not crying "happy tears" before the delivery process was complete. No, that came afterwards, not during. I believe God intends for us to be victorious over our enemies, in those final days. I just cannot imagine He would whisk us off the field, in the middle of the fourth quarter, right when the game is on the line. That doesn't sound like victory to me. It sounds like forfeit, but enough of that for now.

Let's get back to the important stuff, here. I want us to remember that God's promises are true. Our pain and suffering is only for a season. He is preparing an amazing place for His Bride to be able to spend eternity with Him, no doubt. Until then, we may have to endure some trials and tribulations. But, He tells us not to fear. Though we may suffer hardship and pain for a little while, when we get to Heaven, not only will it all be worth it, we won't even remember how bad it was, just as with the woman in His story.

God is so good to us, so very good.

ZOOMING OUT

But what, then, does this parable have to do with "Wedding Preparations," pray tell? I knew you were going to ask and I'm glad you did. Earlier in this section, we talked about Jesus letting the little children come to Him and we learned about the two sons who were asked to work in the field and weren't exactly excited about the proposition. Then we learned about the wealthy man, who invited all the "big shots" to a wedding, and they all were too busy, so he invited all the rest of the people to come.

That led to us talking about Israel becoming a nation, again after two thousand years, and the five wise and foolish virgins who were awaiting the bridegroom. The bottom line is, none of it was easy or without worries or struggles. But God always provided a way. He always will, if we put Him first.

If any of you have ever been involved in planning a wedding, you know that is never easy. There are scheduling issues, food issues, dress issues, guest issues, family issues, and of course, money issues (how are we going to pay for all of this?). Some of the ones I have been around seemed a lot like a "great tribulation," at times. But somehow, when the day arrives, the joy of the moment and seeing these two people who love one another, starting down the path of a brand-new life together, makes all the worry and frustration worthwhile and quickly replaced with happiness and to some degree, relief. Yes, I said it. Relief. . . ahhhh. . . finally!!

No, I cannot say for sure whether we, as Christians, will be taken out of the world before the Great Tribulation starts, or if God plans to "protect us from the evil one" in the midst of it all (although I tend to think the latter more accurately fits in with the rest of what I see in Scripture). But, what I am thoroughly convinced of, is that God loves each and every one of us very much, and it is not His will that any of His children should perish. That is why He sent His Son.

I do believe, however, that no matter what we have to endure in this life, like Noah, like Joseph, like Daniel, like Shadrach, Meshach, Abednego and so many others including Jesus, Himself. God did not abandon them during their times of great trials and testing, the Lord fully intends do what He said in John 17, and that is, protect us from the evil one. That will never change.

I love the old saying, "If God has brought you to it, He will see you through it." I believe that with all my heart.

STORY THIRTY-NINE

"About Abide and Abode"

"I am the true vine, and My Father is the vinedresser. Every branch in Me that does not bear fruit, He takes away; and every branch that bears fruit, He prunes it so that it may bear more fruit. You are already clean because of the word which I have spoken to you. Abide in Me, and I in you. As the branch cannot bear fruit of itself unless it abides in the vine, so neither can you unless you abide in Me. I am the vine, you are the branches; he who abides in Me and I in him, he bears much fruit, for apart from Me you can do nothing." [John 15:1-5]

ZOOMING IN

So, let's see, for those of you who are keeping track, our Master Storyteller has been a winemaker, living water, a physician, a bridegroom, the bread of heaven, a shepherd and now He is referring to Himself as a vine and His Father, a vinedresser. And, that all points to one more strategy frequently used by our Storyteller, one that we haven't talked about yet.

He often used Himself as the main character in His stories. That is not something many like to do. In fact, if there was a storyteller who always made himself the center of his stories, you might say the guy was a bit stuck on himself. "C'mon now, you did this, you are that, yada, yada. We get it...you're amazing!! Sheesh. Why does everything have to be about you?"

Another common thread in His storytelling, one that didn't sit well with many who heard Him, was His insistence on referring to Himself as the Son of God. They were probably saying things like, "Aren't we all children of God? What makes you so special? God has lots of sons and daughters, right? Well okay, there was that one time when you were being baptized and this voice from Heaven was heard saying, *"This is My beloved Son, in whom I am well-pleased." [Matthew 3:17]*

Others might have said, "Alright, fine, I guess we can add Son of God to the list. But does He have to keep rubbing it in our faces? He keeps insisting that we bow down and serve Him, as if He were God and not His Father. Talk about having an ego. Plus, He wants to be treated like God, too. Boy, I'll bet you His Father is going really lay into Him, next time they talk. Getting a little too big for His britches, there, isn't He?"

So, now He refers to Himself as a vine, with His Father being the vinedresser, pruning back the branches that do not bear fruit, so that the remaining ones might produce more. But, He also said they need to be, and stay, "in Him." What does that mean? Shouldn't He be giving His Father more of the credit? Back in Genesis, it was God who told Adam and Eve to *"be fruitful and multiply" [Genesis 1:28]*, right? Why is the Son now taking credit for producing fruit? Yes, we will answer those questions, I promise. But first, I want to point out one other thing that is nagging me about this story.

What is all this talk about "abiding?" That seems to be a peculiar word choice. In this chapter, John 15 (still part of this "Farewell Discourse"), just from verse 4 to verse 10, He uses the word "abide" ten different times. Talk about repetition, this must be important.

The word "abide" is defined in a number of ways. It is a verb that can mean to stay, to remain, to live or to dwell or to draw your existence from. So, yes, it would make sense that the fruit depends on and draws it existence from the vine and that if it is cut off, it will be of no use. Okay, it's pretty important, I guess.

But, I'd like to add to that a little bit. Abide is the verb form of the word abode. I think most of us would be more familiar with that word, right? If someone says to you, "Welcome to my humble abode," you would know they mean their house or place of residence. And we would understand that a home provides safety, warmth, protection, comfort and it comes with a sense of belonging or being connected to something that endures. One could say, you live in an abode, but you abide where you live.

So, to sum up, Jesus is saying the fruit is dependent on being connected to the vine and He is the vine that produces the type of fruit that has eternal benefits, life everlasting. Therefore, staying connected to Him is what is essential to producing life-generating fruit. And, if we remember from the mustard seed story, more fruit produces more seeds that can result in even more fruit. So, with God, there is always a multiplication factor at work. It is never just about me, or you or the guy down the street. It is about us, bearing fruit so that others may become connected to the vine, Jesus Christ, as well, that they might also produce fruit.

And on and on it goes.

ZOOMING OUT

I also do not want us to gloss over the importance of Jesus saying we are to bear fruit "in Him." The Gospel of Jesus Christ is not about flying solo. It is all about relationship. God said in Genesis, *"It is not good for the man to be alone" [Genesis 2:18]* and of course that goes for women, as well. We were all designed and hard-wired to function best within the confines of a healthy relationship, provided we are willing to commit to it.

The primary example of this is marriage. God designed it so that the future of the human race was totally dependent on a man and woman, hopefully within a committed relationship (that's hugely important), producing offspring in their own image, just as God created us in His own image. And the goal is that we would not just reproduce physically, but spiritually, as well. However, that part of the plan ran off the tracks quite quickly, when Adam and Eve believed the lie of the serpent and fell into sin.

I'd like to take this tangent on relationships between a man and a woman down a slightly different path, for a moment if I may. But, before I do, I am going to ask for a little leniency again, as what I am about to share may seem a little sexist, if viewed with modern eyes. I assure you, this is not meant to be sexist at all. God loves women and men equally; I never have doubted it for a second. But I do want to look at how the relationship between the Bride and the Bridegroom, in Scripture, was portrayed. I find it quite fascinating. I hope you will too. I only share this because I believe it is a key to fully understanding this parable.

Let's go back to the Jewish wedding traditions, for a second. A prospective groom identifies a woman he wants to marry. He travels to where she is, from his father's house to her father's house. He not only asks her to marry him, but asks for her father's permission, as well. If the father agrees, they work out an acceptable agreement, which includes a dowry and even a will (in case he dies). Once signed, the father is agreeing to relinquish his daughter to the groom. She is to become his bride and he is become her husband, with all the responsibilities that are assigned to both of them, in their new roles.

When they are officially married, after the groom had gone back home for a year to prepare a dwelling place, or an abode, for them to live in, she will leave her home and go with him to the place he has prepared. At that point, she is very much dependent on him for her safety and well-being. That is what her father agreed to, that the husband would look after and provide for her, just as he did from the time that she was a child.

One might say that her life was now wrapped up in his life, or that in a sense, she was "in Him." Not that she was no longer a separate person, in God's eyes or the eyes of others. She is still an individual, with a life of her own to lead and her own choices to make, that hasn't changed. But the Bible says, *". . . from the beginning of creation, God made them male and female. For this reason, a man shall leave his father and mother, and the two shall become one flesh; so they are no longer two, but one flesh." [Mark 10:6-8]*

What a miracle. God made them individuals first, male and female. That's true. But, when they leave Mom and Dad and enter into marriage, they are no longer just individuals in the eyes of God. He also sees them as *"one flesh."* One flesh, just as the grape is one flesh with the branch and the branch is one flesh with the vine. The grape does not pretend to be the branch nor does the branch pretend to be a grape. No, they have different (yet equally important) roles to fulfill. A branch does not eventually become fruit. And a grape does not show up one day all by itself, without the help of the branch and the vine.

Are we seeing, now, why this might be considered a wedding story? The bride is now drawing her existence from her connection to the groom. And we, as God's people, are the bride, the precious fruit that only finds life in the vine, Jesus Christ.

You see, the entire underlying story, not just in the parables, but in the entire Bible from Genesis through Revelation, is about relationship. God is not a loner. There are three parts, the Father, the Son and the Holy Spirit. Jesus said, *"I am in the Father and the Father is in Me." [John 14:11]*

They all are part of the Godhead and they are all equally God, yet there is an order and a structure to their relationship. In the same way, we are meant to be in relationship, with God and with others. And that means becoming intertwined and interdependent upon each other, to a certain degree. It is truly only because of your sinful nature, that we struggle with relationships. God craves relationships and we were made in His image. We should too.

We can try to be separate and unaccountable to anyone else. It sounds cool, to be your own man or your own woman. But, it doesn't usually work out so well, for we were designed and made to function best within the framework of godly relationships. Husbands and wives, parents and children, church-goers and pastors, employers and employees, citizens and governments.

They are all relationships and God desires us to learn from and find value in our relationships, although at times it may seem like relationships were a really bad idea.

I hear ya.

STORY FORTY

"The Readied Bride Arrives"

And a voice came from the throne, saying, "Give praise to our God, all you His bond-servants, you who fear Him, the small and the great." Then I heard something like the voice of a great multitude and like the sound of many waters and like the sound of mighty peals of thunder, saying, "Hallelujah! For the Lord our God, the Almighty, reigns. Let us rejoice and be glad and give the glory to Him, for the marriage of the Lamb has come and His bride has made herself ready." It was given to her to clothe herself in fine linen, bright and clean; for the fine linen is the righteous acts of the saints. Then he said to me, "Write, 'Blessed are those who are invited to the marriage supper of the Lamb.'" And he said to me, "These are true words of God." [Revelation 19:5-9]

First of all, let me add my "Hallelujah," as we have finally arrived at the last step on our forty-story journey through the Parables of Jesus. It has been a long journey, but one that I have thoroughly enjoyed. I only hope you have, too. Looking at these stories up close and with an eye to how they connect has been very revealing. I honestly wasn't quite sure where it would end up. But, as is so often the case with our Lord, it has certainly surpassed my expectations. Thanks for hanging in there with me. I know we wandered around in the desert a bit (only for forty stories, or so). But, here we are. This is where it all comes together, I hope!!

Back in Story One, if you remember, I wandered outside of the accepted lines of what is considered a parable and what is not, as we looked at the Wedding at Cana and Jesus turning the water into wine. I considered it a "wordless parable," but a parable, no less. I believe the Lord was using that miracle, a side story, to announce that "All things had become new." So, you might not be surprised that I am going to take similar liberties, here in Story Forty, as we look at another wedding, the long-awaited "marriage of the Lamb." Amen and Hallelujah, indeed. We started off with a wedding story, so it's only fitting that end with one.

We, also, started off this journey with three stories from the gospel of John. So, what do you know, the last three stories are also from the pen of "the Disciple whom Jesus loved" (that is how John would refer to himself in his writings, so as to not use his own name). But, this last one is from John's vision recorded in Revelation Chapter 19, regarding this long-awaited wedding and the revealing of the Lamb's "readied bride."

ZOOMING IN

For this story, and to explain why I have included it in a book about the parables, I think it is best that I start off with my conclusion. Then, I can go on and explain how I got there. The reason I included this short passage from John, about the "Marriage Supper of the Lamb," is because I think it is only a side story (of sorts), an illustration if you will, of what is really happening in this glorious vision. It is really not all that different than the miracle Jesus performed at the Wedding at Cana. It was a fitting illustration of something much greater. In my book, that qualifies as a parable, or side story, which is what a parable is.

I believe that from the beginning of time (remember, *"In the beginning was the Word, and the Word was with God, and the Word was God," [John 1:1],* all things were pointing towards this culmination of the joining of Jesus Christ and His chosen ones into a covenant relationship that would have no end. But we, being bound by our earthly limitations and perceptions, are not fully able to comprehend all that will be unfolding in Heaven on that day. So, portraying it as a wedding feast was the best illustration God could use, I think, to help us grasp the immense gravity and significance of this upcoming event. When I say it will be "out of this world," that might be one of the few times the phrase was ever used properly. It will definitely be "other-worldly," and I thank God for that.

But, let's talk through some of the similarities between the Jewish wedding traditions we talked about and what our Lord Jesus did, in preparation for coming to this blessed event:

1.   He found the one that He loved, Israel (and later we, the church, were grafted in). And He persued her relentlessly, even when she was less than faithful towards Him.

2.   He left His Father's house and came to where she lived, to ask for her hand in marriage.

3.   He negotiated an appropriate price for the dowry (His life and blood) and made a promise to come back for her at the appropriate time.

4.   While He has been away, He has been preparing a place for them to enjoy together, forever, once that marriage becomes official.

5.   The bride has been making herself ready and living as a betrothed woman, keeping herself pure and awaiting His return. Remember the "mikvah", the pool where the bride took a ceremonial bath to make herself ready? It is very similar to the Christian tradition of baptism, where we are ceremonially submerged in the water, to signify we are made clean for Him, as well.

6.   And, of course, our Lord held up His end of the bargain by paying the dowry in full, at the Cross of Calvary, and He is now preparing for His promised return.

7.   Lastly, remember that the Jews consider a wedding to be a sort of Yom Kippur, a time of repentance and forgiveness. That is hugely important in all of this, I would say. In fact, it is primarily what it is all about. Forgiveness, repentance, redemption and, last but not least, true, unfailing love. If a marriage is going to last, it is important to start off with a clean slate, no secrets and no regrets. Christ provided that.

All that is left, at this point, is the fulfillment of His return and the taking away of the bride, back to His Father's house and the place where the wedding feast will take place. And our part in it, you might be wondering, is to simply "accept His proposal" and begin to ready ourselves to meet Him, when He returns. The guest list has been prepared (the Book of Life) and the invitations have been sent (the preaching of the Gospel to the whole Earth).

Our job then, as believers, is to remain pure to Him and make sure we have enough oil for our lamps to keep them lit brightly until the day He arrives to take us home. By keeping our lamps brightly lit, you see, it will also attract the attention of others who would love to attend this wedding, as well. And they are WELCOME!!

ZOOMING OUT

This may be the toughest parable of all for me to wrap up, since I need to adequately bring together all the loose ends from this journey, without the chapter becoming thirty pages long. But, I will try my best. I promise.

It seems to me that ever since the world was formed, and even before that, God desired to be joined in covenant (a promise without end) to those who would choose to commit to love Him forever. The keyword, there, is "choose." We all have been given "free will." God will never force us to love Him. It's not love if it is not freely given. He wanted a bride who, even in the face of great temptation to choose otherwise, was willing to make a vow to love Him, be with Him forever and seek no other.

So yes, reluctantly, He allowed sin into the world to provide a different path, knowing that some would choose to go in the other direction. But, again, it really wouldn't be a true choice, if there were not tempting alternatives. If there were only one woman in the world, or one man, to choose from, it wouldn't be much of a commitment to vow to be true only to them, right?

So, as much as it hurt Him to do so, He allowed for sin to run its course, with all the pain and suffering that goes with it, to make sure He was not rigging things in His favor, so to speak. The choices had to be real and unmanipulated by God, Himself. Otherwise, they would not be real alternatives.

He also made sure, through His Son, Jesus Christ, that adequate payment was made to cover all the sins of every person who has ever lived. . . past, present and future. He needed to make sure that if, and when, they saw the error of their ways and called on His name, unconditional forgiveness would be available and sufficient.

Do you remember the parable about the wedding feast, where the rich man said, **"Go out to the streets and invite everyone else."** Make no mistake about. Everyone is invited. No exceptions, whether we accept the invitation or not. That is up to the individual. Again, no one will be forced to attend. It is not a "shotgun wedding." It's a wedding where the two parties are marrying for the only right reason there is. LOVE.

And, this is a marriage that will never, never, ever end in divorce. All sin and temptation will be no more, at that point. It will not be permitted into the Lamb's Kingdom. That, is why the bride must be "made ready." Sin is not permitted there. And anyone who has not been washed, not just in a ceremonial pool of water, but in the blood of the Lamb, will not be admitted.

That is one of the most incredible attributes of God, if you ask me. He cannot be tricked or fooled. No one, on that day, will be able to talk their way in, or buy their way in, or sneak in a back door, somehow. God knows our every thought, our every word and every intention of our heart. Only those who have entered through Christ and His sacrifice will be present. And each of the names of all those who will accept His proposal, are already written in the Lamb's Book of Life (even if they have not done so yet, He knows who will). The guest list has been checked, double-checked and verified. Jesus is the only door. He is the only truth and the only way. No one comes to the father, but by Him, as it says in John 14:6. But here is the good news:

But as many as received Him, to them He gave the right to become children of God, even to those who believe in His name, who were born, not of blood nor of the will of the flesh nor of the will of man, but of God. [John 1:12-13]

It is totally up to us receive Him, as an individual, no one will force you to. Just as no one should force someone to marry, as they did in the old days. Marriage should be a choice, mutually made by two parties, motivated by love and only love. It should not be a choice made because of looks, wealth, convenience or even the wishes of the family. It is purely an individual's decision to make. And no one can, or should, make it for them. That is not love.

One other thing of great importance to mention here, while the sacrifice Christ made was sufficient for every person who has ever lived to find forgiveness and mercy, it is a "limited time offer." Maybe we will not be alive when Christ returns for His bride. Maybe we will be. But, all of us are going to run out of time, here on Earth, at some point. In the Book of Hebrews, these words were written:

And inasmuch as it is appointed for men to die once and after this comes judgment, so Christ also, having been offered once to bear the sins of many, will appear a second time for salvation without reference to sin, to those who eagerly await Him. [Hebrews 9:27]

When that last breath is breathed, the time for decisions will have passed. Christ is coming again for those who have put their faith and trust in Him as their Lord and Savior. Will you be among those who *"eagerly awaited Him,"* (as the Scripture says) and are standing in the presence of our Lord, when the "wedding of all weddings" finally arrives?

I truly hope that you are. Because, it is at that appointed time and place, chosen by God the Father, Himself, that the "readied bride" will be revealed, for all to see.

And, oh, and what a beautiful bride she will be.

All praise and honor to the One *"who is, and who was and is to come, the Almighty." [Revelation 1:8]*

CONCLUSION

"Happily Ever After"

Once upon a time, a man came into this world who loved to tell stories. Oh, no, not in a bad way, but rather in a very good way. His stories often revealed much about who He was. In fact, there were times that He intentionally made Himself the main character. What was interesting about these stories, beyond the stories themselves (which were quite interesting), is that they revealed much about the people who were hearing these stories, as well. Sometimes, the listeners were inspired and comforted by these stories, but often they were troubled. Some even became angry.

Stories have the potential to do that. They can make you laugh, make you cry, make you happy, or even very unhappy or mad. A good story is one that can make you feel many emotions, at different points in the story. But the great ones usually have a happy ending. Sometimes this is called "redeeming (or resolving) the storyline." A writer or storyteller rarely wants to leave things hanging, at the end. Unless, of course, there is a sequel in the works. In that case, you might plan on having a hanging ending.

In this book, we looked at forty individual parables with the hopes of seeing how they might connect to one another. It was my goal to search for a larger or underlying storyline that painted a greater picture. Much like the pixels in a digital photograph, that when joined together, reveal something much larger and hopefully more beautiful. That is what I was zooming in on.

I am happy to say that I believe we have succeeded. And what has been uncovered, during our journey, was quite surprising.

I believe it was no accident that the first miracle that Jesus performed was at a wedding, the turning of water into wine.

Although, that may not have been a parable, in the usual sense, it was a side story that was pointing to the larger story, I believe.

Jesus had arrived, as promised, and His arrival changed everything. All things, through Him, had become new. We saw water become wine, in the blink of an eye. A Jewish priest was told of a new type of birth, a second birth, if you will. A woman heard Him talk of a new type of water, one that quenches your thirst, permanently.

But, He was also pointing to a new way of interacting with God, much to the displeasure of the religious and political leaders of the day. They liked things just the way they were. Why wouldn't they? They were in control. The arrival of Jesus Christ signaled the end of their uncontested authority. And they did not like it one bit.

Think of a situation where a daughter has taken an interest in a boy, but not the type of boy the family had in mind for her. When things start to get serious, they begin to get worried and even try to find ways to cause them to split up.

That is what the Jewish leaders were feeling, back then. They were afraid that their people, their flock, their meal-ticket, might fall in love with this guy and run off and get married. They were not about to let that happen. But, little did they know, there was nothing they could do to stop it. There was going to be a wedding, even if they did not approve. They just did not know it yet.

Meanwhile, the people were confused, maybe even torn. They were intrigued by what Jesus had to say, but it went against just about everything they believed their whole lives. The last thing they wanted to do was disrespect their father's wishes. But, what if their father was wrong. What if God was initiating these changes?

When Jesus spoke about the Kingdom of Heaven, in their hearts, they believed what He was saying was true. They wanted to believe it. But, many were afraid to, because it would likely bring the wrath of the "powers that be" down on them. Even their own families would be upset with them. What were they to do?

But, they believed that Jesus loved them, and they were beginning to truly love Him, as well. He was healing the sick, restoring sight to the blind, even raising the dead. They were finding it very hard to believe that this man was not from God. After all, God, through His prophets, had long promised that a Redeemer, a Messiah, would one day come to rescue them and establish His Kingdom. Was this the Promised One? Many were starting to believe, He was. Little did they know, He was not just coming to save His people. He was looking for His Bride, a bride unlike any other.

Jesus had come down from Heaven, from His Father's house, with good news in His hand, which was a marriage proposal. Who doesn't get excited when an engagement is announced? That is almost always good news, unless your daughter is going to marry the boy from "the other side of the tracks." Unfortunately, that is what the Jews were thinking. They didn't like this "good news" at all.

He came with the permission of the Father and with the dowry and contract already agreed to. He was ready to pay the dowry and return to His Father's house, to begin preparing their "forever home." All the bride had to do was accept the proposal and make herself ready. All she had to do was say, "Yes."

If this decision was not tough enough, this perspective groom may not have been what the family and friends had been hoping for, but He was a prince who would someday be not just a king, but the King of kings. And the palace that He was preparing was beyond comprehension. So, what was the problem? Why did so many not see it? They were blinded by their own desires, their own agendas. They couldn't see past the tips of their own noses. What a tragedy. Would they really pass on a chance at eternity, refuse the new wine, just because they had become so attached to the old wine? Sadly, many did.

And if we are to believe the Bible, many more will. This story was just not about the Jews and the Gentiles from two thousand years ago. This story is also a modern tale, an interactive one if you will, with us as central characters. The choice is ours to make, every bit as much as it was Peter's or Paul's...or even Herod's.

So, tell me, what will you do? The Good News of the Gospel of Jesus Christ is basically a marriage proposal. I believe it was meant to be just that, from the beginning of time (talk about a long engagement). He wants you to not just agree to be His bride (for all the wrong reasons). No, He wants you to desire to be with Him for all eternity, with all of your heart. And He desires to be with you, for all eternity, as well. So much so, He is already preparing that future abode (you knew I would get that in there, didn't you)? And here is how the Apostle Paul describes it:

"THINGS WHICH EYE HAS NOT SEEN AND EAR HAS NOT HEARD, AND WHICH HAVE NOT ENTERED THE HEART OF MAN, ALL THAT GOD HAS PREPARED FOR THOSE WHO LOVE HIM."
[1 Corinthians 2:9]

Yeah, it's going to be all that and much, much more. Forget all about the "Wedding of the Century." This is going to be the "Wedding of All Weddings." And you are not just invited. No, you have been asked to be part of His eternal Bride, to become His beloved.

It might be understandable for someone to say, "No," to the Gospel of Jesus Christ. That is not something most people fully understand. To many, it sounds like "finding religion" or "trading your brain for a Bible."

But, it is actually a marriage proposal from the King of Kings to little ol' you and little ol' me. He wants to be permanently joined to you, forever and ever. He wants to protect you and keep you and give you the desires or your heart. He wants to be there in good times and bad, in sickness and in health. Only there will be no more sickness, death or parting. It is truly a "neverending love story."

What would you say to that?

As the headwater said, at the Wedding of Cana.....

"...you have kept the good wine until now!!" [John 2:10]

Isn't that just like God, to save the best for last?

Especially, when the best will last forever.

The End.

About The Author

I included this picture, here, because it fit so well with the theme of this book. Pictured here, are the results of my thirty-nine years of marriage. If children are a blessing from the Lord, I'm really blessed!! Lauri Lee and I have four children and seven (soon to be eight) grandchildren. And they all live nearby us, here in Northeast Ohio, where we have lived our whole lives. God is so good!!

For more than fifty years, music has been the primary avenue for my creativity, as a musician, singer and songwriter. I have written and recorded well over two hundred songs, in various genres, from Pop and Rock, Modern Country and, of course, Contemporary Christian music and Worship music...and I still do that today.

But now, God has nudged me to do a different kind of writing, He has asked me to share what I have learned, over the last thirty-eight years, as a Christian, by writing books that help others come to know Christ, as well. I only hope you have enjoyed this walk through the Parables as much as I did researching and writing it. Thank you so much for coming along. God's blessings to you!!

Bob Palumbo

Let's keep the conversation going:

EMAIL: unlockingcreation@gmail.com

TWITTER: @bobsbooktalk

BLOG: unlockingcreation.wordpress.com

Research Sources

The Ryrie Study Bible (New American Standard
Version)www.biblegateway.com

www.biblehub.com

www.swapmeetdave.com/Bible/Parables

www.biblehistory.com

www.jewishweddingtraditions.com

www.gotquestions.org

(All Bible verses are from the New American Standard)

ADDITIONAL NOTES